MINNESOTA LOGGING RAILROADS

A Pictorial History of the Era
When White Pine and the Logging Railroad
Reigned Supreme

Frank A. King

Golden West Books
San Marino, California

MINNESOTA LOGGING RAILROADS

Copyright © 1981 by Frank A. King
All Rights Reserved
Published by Golden West Books
San Marino, California 91108 U.S.A.
Library of Congress Card No. 81-6940
I.S.B.N. 0-87095-076-2

Library of Congress Cataloging in Publication Data

King, Frank Alexander, 1923-
    Minnesota logging railroads.

    Bibliography: p.
    Includes index.
    1. Logging railroads—Minnesota—History.   I. Title.
TF24.M6K56   385′.54′09776   81-6940
ISBN 0-87095-076-2   AACR2

ACKNOWLEDGEMENTS

No one writes a book like *Minnesota Logging Railroads* without the unselfish assistance of countless people. There are writers who have recorded their research in published books; there are libraries and archives of records, historical data and photographs taken nearly a hundred years ago. A complete acknowledgment would be impossible.

I wish to particularly express appreciation to the Bemidji State University Library, the Carlton County Historical Society, the Chippewa County Historical Society, the Crow Wing County Historical Society, the Koochiching County Historical Society, the St. Louis County Historical Society and the Thunder Bay Historical Society (Canada) for making available their archives and photographic collections. Special thanks is extended to the Minnesota Historical Society for generous use of their vast photographic and archival materials.

For their contribution of photographs I extend thanks to Pete Bonesteel, Herbert L. Broadbelt, Dr. Richard Brown, John Fritzen, Benjamin F. G. Kline, Jr., Wayne C. Olsen, James C. Ryan, L. R. Schrenk, Paul Silliman, Dr. Charles Vandersluis and Dr. Carl A. Zapffe. I am grateful to Gerald M. Best for his assistance in reviewing the locomotive rosters of long forgotten logging railroads.

Appreciation is extended to Thomas Hoff, James P. Kaysen, Howard Peddle and Donald B. Shank for their review of the manuscript and valuable suggestions.

Finally I offer thanks to Donald Duke, publisher of Golden West Books for his time and effort in presenting this material in book form. He has spent countless hours blending the text with the illustrations. Also to Harlan Hiney for the jacket and end paper illustrations, and Glen W. Burke for his maps. Lastly, the patience and understanding shown by my wife and family during the various stages of completing this book.

End Paper Illustration
A Mitchell & McClure logging railroad train steams across the bridge spanning the Black Hoof near Duluth. This immense structure, constructed entirely out of logs, was almost 750 feet long and stood over 100 feet high at the river. This rendering by railroad artist Harlan Hiney was made from a cut appearing in the February 1, 1895 issue of the *Mississippi Valley Lumberman.*

Golden West Books

A Division of Pacific Railroad Publications, Inc.

P.O. BOX 8136 • SAN MARINO, CALIFORNIA • 91108

Dedicated to the rugged breed of men
who built and operated
the logging railroads

PREFACE

Minnesota's colorful era of logging and lumbering, as well as its rise and decline as one of the nation's leading lumber producers, are well documented. Such accounts have naturally focused on the romantic life of the lumberjack, on logging methods, river drives, and mills. While Minnesota's logging railroads have been mentioned in passing, their importance as a major mode of transportation has never been accorded proper recognition. The purpose of this book is to do justice to this interesting aspect of the state's once great lumber industry.

It was only logical to conduct the earliest logging activities along rivers and streams, making use of the sleigh haul and river drive for log transportation. Within a short time, however, timber stands convenient to water transportation were depleted, and it became obvious to lumbermen that the era of easy and comparatively inexpensive logging was over. Taking a page from the book of their counterparts in Michigan and Wisconsin, men who had reached this point in their operations some years earlier, set the stage for the introduction into Minnesota of logging railroads. From a modest beginning — J.M. Paine's logging railroad, begun in 1886 and located approximately 20 miles west of Duluth — logging railroads during the next three decades spread like wildfire through the northern part of the state.

Before the boom ended, some 40 logging and lumbering companies, including the biggest names in the industry, constructed an estimated 5,000 miles of logging railroad lines within Minnesota! Operation of such railroads, many of which became common carriers of substantial proportions, required the service of some 230 locomotives and 4,800 log cars. These figures are exclusive of the equipment employed by major first class roads which also engaged in logging operations along their lines, e.g., Duluth & Iron Range; Duluth, Missabe & Northern; Great Northern; and Northern Pacific.

Logging railroads provided Minnesota lumbermen with a means of breaking away from traditional transportation patterns by moving logs in directions nature had never intended. Most important, however, was the fact that logs could now move to sawmills year round, thus maximizing the use of those expensive facilities.

From a conservation standpoint, logging railroads were a negative phenomenon. Inasmuch as the investment involved in constructing and equipping them amounted to a substantial percentage of the total cost of producing lumber, their coming promoted a policy of "cut out and get out." Moreover, the existing tax structure in Minnesota failed to promote selective cutting, with the end result that few if any companies could afford a policy of retention and maintenance of forests for future timber harvesting. This situation, coupled with the state requirement that slashings be burned, spelled the end of the white pine industry in Minnesota.

Had the development of a reliable motor truck come about earlier, the logging railroad map of Minnesota would certainly have looked drastically different. Approximately 3,000 miles of logging spurs would never have been constructed. Instead, logging trucks would have performed the gathering service in the woods, eventually reloading logs onto rail cars for the long haul to the mill, a combination method of operation adopted as standard by most West Coast loggers later in this century.

Happily, portions of main line trackage initially constructed for logging interests remain in operation today. These consist of the Burlington Northern line between Brainerd and International Falls, which began as Minnesota's only narrow-gauge logging railroad, and the Duluth, Winnipeg & Pacific line between Virginia and Fort Frances, Ontario, which currently constitutes an extremely important segment of a route between western Canada and the midwestern United States via the lake ports of Duluth and Superior.

While exploring or trout fishing in the jungle-like environment north of Lake Superior, this writer has run across traces of the old logging railroads which once blanketed the area. One may still stumble over a rusted angle iron, a brakeshoe, or even a short section of 40-pound rail — all signs of a vanished right-of-way. At times, an electronic metal detector, signalling the location of spikes and other iron, has proven invaluable in finding old grades. Diligent search will occasionally reveal a cut or fill, with trees up to two feet in diameter growing where once the ground shook under the weight of steam locomotives and strings of loaded log cars.

Frank A. King

Duluth, Minnesota
June 1981

TABLE OF CONTENTS

Old Lizzie about ready to depart Mud Lake Camp for the J. M. Paine mill at Carlton. The man in the center with his hands behind his back is William Shields, the foreman. This 1887 vintage Shay was sold to a logging concern in British Columbia around the turn of the century. — JOHN FRITZEN COLLECTION

1

BEGINNINGS IN MINNESOTA

The American lumber industry was born in Maine and moved progressively across the country on the heels of the nation's westward expansion. The first reliable statistics about it, which appeared in the 1840 census, indicated a total annual production of about 1½ billion board feet. By then, New York State had become the leading producer, with Pennsylvania running a close second.

In 1860, total lumber production rose to 8 billion board feet. The leading states then were Pennsylvania, New York, Ohio, Indiana, Michigan, Maine, and Virginia, in that order. Within the next few years, the pine forests in the East were almost exhausted, and Maine lumbermen turned their eyes toward the seemingly "inexhaustible" forest of white pine in "the Lake States" — their term for Michigan, Wisconsin, and Minnesota.

America's lumber production, in 1870, totaled approximately 13 billion board feet, with Michigan in first place, trailed by Pennsylvania, New York, Wisconsin, Indiana, and Maine. Ten years later, Michigan mills produced approximately 4.2 billion board feet of lumber, at a time when the Lake States accounted for 35 percent of the total production, surpassing the entire output of all the eastern states.

In 1890, Michigan was still the leading lumber state, Wisconsin ran a close second, however, and in 1899 took over the top position with an annual production of almost 3.5 billion board feet, valued at $57,634,000. Michigan fell to second place, with just over 3 billion board feet, valued at $54,000,000. Minnesota ranked third, with 2.3 billion board feet that brought in $43,000,000, and was followed by Pennsylvania, Arkansas, and Washington.

By the late 1880's, lumbermen had begun looking for new sources of logs to supplement Michigan's and Wisconsin's dwindling reserves. Naturally, they were attracted by neighboring Minnesota, where great timber reserves stood virtually untapped. Minnesota contained the last vast stand of white pine in the Lake States. Centrally located therein were some 5,000 square miles of hardwoods, while to the north were immense stands of white and Norway pine on high ground, with cedar, spruce, and tamarack in the swampy areas. For the most part, the pine was located to the north and east of the Mississippi River, and extended unbroken to the Canadian border, Minnesota's pine areas were slightly larger than Michigan's and about 30 percent larger than Wisconsin's. Unfortunately, a large portion of the timber proved of inferior quality.

In Minnesota, as in Michigan and Wisconsin, the earliest logging activities took place along rivers, down which logs could be floated to the mills. The

Early logging scene in the Duluth area. Motive power for skidding logs to the railroad was provided by a yoke of oxen. — FRANK KING COLLECTION

A massive log jam on the St. Croix River at Taylors Falls, Minnesota, in 1888. This particular jam contained an estimated 200,000,000 board feet. The St. Croix was an important artery during early logging in Minnesota and Wisconsin — MINNESOTA HISTORICAL SOCIETY

Logs owned by various owners were sorted out at this sorting works on the St. Croix River as shown in this 1886 scene. Ownership identification was made possible by a stamp mark driven into each end of the log. — MINNESOTA HISTORICAL SOCIETY

This sleigh load of logs contained 62 logs totaling 21,507 board feet. This scene was photographed at Clark & Jackson Camp No. 1 about 20 miles west of Duluth on March 19, 1899. — CARLTON COUNTY HISTORICAL SOCIETY

first large-scale logging was conducted along the St. Croix, Rum, and other tributaries of the Mississippi. Soon, however, most of those stands convenient to river banking and driving were depleted. Large pine areas still awaiting the ring of the axe lay to the north; but reaching this timber presented unique problems not generally encountered in Michigan or Wisconsin. Northern Minnesota terrain became increasingly rugged and uncompromising. Many of the streams there were subject to rapid run-off and thus not suitable for log driving. It became apparent that other methods of log transportation would have to be introduced in order to remove timber beyond reach of navigable streams. In some instances, small mills were located close to timber stands and horse-drawn sleighs used for transportation; however, this represented at best only a temporary solution to the problem, since transport activity was limited to winter months and the haul restricted to approximately five to six miles. It did not take lumbermen long to evaluate and justify the construction of logging railroads. Once they were in operation, expensive sawmills would no longer have to stand idle because of an early spring thaw that put an end to sleigh hauling or for a lack of run-off water to drive logs by river.

13

Narrow-gauge No. 1, a Mason Bogie type locomotive, on Hovey & McCracken's logging railroad came to Michigan from Colorado's famed Denver, South Park & Pacific Railroad. — C. T. STONER COLLECTION

In Michigan, the first logging railroad had come into being in 1874. George and Hugh Campbell of Bay City constructed the standard gauge Pinconning & Lake Shore Railroad to transport logs to the mills at Pinconning and finished lumber to Saginaw Bay. Its success was evidenced by the rapid increase in the number of such roads. By 1885, there were 71 individual logging railroads in that state, operating over some 500 miles of trackage, using 110 locomotives and approximately 2,000 cars.

Local legend and an official Wisconsin State Historical Society marker proclaims that Wisconsin's first logging railroad was constructed by Frederick Weyerhaeuser about 30 miles north of the lumbering community of Chippewa Falls during the winter of 1875-1876. The plaque is located along the site of the old Chippewa River & Menomonie Railway at Weyerhaeuser, and there was no reason to question this official statement.

In the preparation of the locomotive rosters, located in the appendix section of this book, the author asked Gerald M. Best one of the country's foremost locomotive historians to check his official builders construction records with the authors information. The official H.K. Porter records indicate that the first locomotive built for the Chippewa River & Menomonie Railway was not completed at the builder's factory until February of 1883. At once this left the author with some doubt concerning the validity of the 1875-1876 date mentioned above. An ex-

The narrow-gauge log train, shown on the opposite page in the upper view, was photographed on the Welch Lake Branch of the Crescent Springs Railroad as it steamed towards the mill at Shell Lake, Wisconsin. Construction of the Cresent Springs Railroad began in 1881 making it the earliest logging railroad in Wisconsin. Engine No. 2, a woodburning Baldwin Mogul, was acquired secondhand in 1881. — HOWARD PEDDLE COLLECTION (LOWER RIGHT) The same engine at Shell Lake. Note the "Big Wheels" on flat cars which were used in area logging. — FRANK KING COLLECTION

The Chippewa River & Menomonie, Wisconsin's second logging railroad, was constructed by Weyerhaeuser during the winter of 1883. Spanking new, and sunflower-stacked, this Porter Mogul No. 2 spots a train for unloading at the dump trestle at the "Big Bend" on the Chippewa River during 1884. The writer's father, George R. King, recalled fishing off the abandoned trestle during the early 1890's. — DR. R. C. BROWN COLLECTION

haustive search of the old newspaper files at Chippewa Falls revealed conclusively that the Chippewa River & Menomonie Railway was not in operation until the late spring of 1883. Local legend and the official State plaque have been wrong for some time.

Wisconsin's first logging railroad is now the Crescent Springs Railroad Company constructed during 1881 at Shell Lake. The narrow-gauge (three-foot) line was a subsidiary of the Shell Lake Lumber Company and operated for approximately 20 years. During the time the logging railroad laid some 84 miles of trackage and operated with two Mogul-type locomotives and a fleet of 70 Russel logging cars. About 30 million board feet of logs were carried annually from the woods to the mill at Shell Lake. Interestingly, the lack of driving streams, coupled with terrain unsuited for sleigh hauling, brought about what is now considered as Wisconsin's first logging railroad.

Frederick Weyerhaeuser owned vast timber tracts north of Chippewa Falls, in the vicinity of Potato Lake, near what is now Weyerhaeuser, Wisconsin. He formed the Chippewa Lumber & Boom Company to log his tracts. The company planned to use Potato Lake as a log reservoir and, with the onset of the spring thaw, drive the logs down Potato Creek to the Big Bend on the Chippewa River and then on to the big mill at Chippewa Falls. Unfortunately, in the spring of 1882, company loggers were chagrined to find the creek too shallow and crooked for driving

logs, even with the assistance of supplementary back-up water provided by three dams. These were the events leading up to and the reason for construction of the Chippewa River & Menomonie Railway, Wisconsin's second logging railroad.

Weyerhaeuser was faced with the dilemma of a lake filled with logs and no water-borne method of moving them to his mill. He likely recalled the successful operation of the logging railroad operated by the Shell Lake Lumber Company, in which he had a financial interest, considering a railroad as a more expensive but practical solution to the problem. During the winter that followed, he had 45-pound rails, logging cars, and a small Porter 0-4-2 type saddle-tank locomotive hauled overland on sleighs from Chippewa Falls to Potato Lake. Here he built a standard gauge railroad approximately six miles in length to haul the logs from Potato Lake to a landing at the Big Bend of the Chippewa.

It was during the decade of the 1870's that Ephriam Shay, a Michigan logger, came a cropper of events of nature. As it happened, an open winter left Shay's logs in the woods right where they had been cut. Then and there, he determined to divorce himself from the uncertainties of horse and sleigh operations, a decision which resulted in the creation of the Shay-geared locomotive, a rugged machine that would come to be synonymous with railroad logging all over the world for more than half a century.

In Minnesota, the first logging railroad appeared during 1886. Constructed by J.M. Paine & Company at a cost of $60,000, this line connected the Paine mill at Northern Pacific Junction now known as Carlton (approximately 20 miles west of Duluth) with pine stands some five to ten miles distant. At this time, Michigan boasted the greatest logging railroad mileage of any other state. Comparative statistics of Lake States logging railroads for 1887, including Minnesota's single railroad, read as follows:

State	Roads	No. of Miles of Track Operated Standard-Ga.	Narrow-Ga.	Loco-motives	Cars
Michigan	89	172.5	469	127	2375
Wisconsin	11	81.5	10	18	326
Minnesota	1*	5.0	—	1**	9**

*J.M. Paine & Company
**One year later, the company owned three locomotives and 25 logging cars.

All these early logging railroads were relatively short. In 1887 they averaged only seven or eight miles in length. In nearly every case, they were merely a substitution for horse-drawn sleighs, running between the woods and the banking area along the river.

J.M. Paine's logging railroad, extending from his sawmill at Carlton into the pine of Silver Brook Township, was similar in most respects to those already operating in Michigan and Wisconsin. Within a short time mill output increased to 120,000 board feet per day. This finished lumber, largely railroad

Workmen constructing a trestle on the J. M. Paine logging railroad during the late 1880's. — MINNESOTA HISTORICAL SOCIETY (BELOW) The Shay geared locomotive was the creation of Michigan logger, Ephriam Shay. This photo of a two-truck, three-cylinder Shay was reputedly taken near Cadillac, Michigan, about 1884, and the inventors name appears on the cab. This engine was constructed for demonstration purposes and later sold to the St. Croix Land & Lumber Company in Wisconsin in 1885. — U.S. FOREST SERVICE

Narrow-gauge train on the Washburn & Northwestern Railway dumping logs at Washburn, Wisconsin. The road was one of 11 logging railroads in Wisconsin when construction started in 1887. At the time of this photograph in 1902, the 50 miles of railroad, along with the sawmill at Washburn, had just been acquired by Edward Hines from Bigelow Brothers of Chicago. Just 7 short years later, Hines would become involved in Minnesota's largest lumbering venture, the Virginia & Rainy Lake Company. — MINNESOTA HISTORICAL SOCIETY

and bridge timbers, necessitated the operation of three trains daily to the mill, each made up of eight Russel log cars and carrying a total of approximately 40,000 board feet of logs. Motive power consisted of an old hand-me-down engine of the American type (4-4-0) dating to pre-Civil War times, a four-wheeled Porter 0-4-0 similar to the famed *Minnetonka* (and likely one of the first four locomotives built for the Northern Pacific in 1870), and a spanking new 28-ton Shay, affectionately referred to as *Lizzie*. The light rails that eventually extended some ten miles from the mill into the woods were utilized until the turn of the century.

Before long, logging railroads penetrated even the most inaccessible timber areas of northern Minnesota, making possible the marketing of timber far removed from navigable waters. For one short era, they played a vital role in transporting vast stands of timber to the mills for conversion into the fresh lumber that supported the expanding farm and urban populations of the midwestern United States during the early years of our own century.

By making it possible to move logs where nature never intended them to go, the logging railroad broke traditional transportation patterns. Logs in the Rainy River drainage area could now move south by rail to the upper Mississippi River like the logs cut along the western portion of the Mesabi Range. Even logs close to the Red River were often railed to the Mississippi instead. One interesting example of the

time was the Taber Lumber Company of Keokuk, Iowa, which in 1902 received a portion of its log supply from an area approximately 12 miles north of the Mesabi Range. The logs were loaded onto cars of the Duluth, Virginia & Rainy Lake Railway and moved to Virginia for interchange with the Great Northern. The cars were handled over the Great Northern to Cloquet, where they were turned over to the Northern Pacific, hauled over the old St. Paul & Duluth road to Stillwater, and dumped. From Stillwater, the logs were rafted down the St. Croix and Mississippi rivers to Keokuk.

A somewhat similar situation involved logs cut along the Mesabi during the late 1890's and destined for mills in Muscatine, Iowa. In this case, the logs were railed by the Mesabi Southern some 30 miles south to the St. Louis River, floated down river to a point below Cloquet, loaded onto rail cars again, and moved over the St. Paul & Duluth to Stillwater, where they were once more placed in the water for rafting to Muscatine.

Lumbermen quickly recognized the advantages of logging by railroad. Rail transport freed the logger from climatic influences and also enabled him to take better advantage of market conditions. Logs could now be cut and hauled to the mills for conversion to lumber on short notice, thereby avoiding tying up substantial capital long in advance of production and sales.

During 1888, in a flowery editorial titled "A

J. M. Paine Company's camp crew and their Shay named *Lizzie* pose for a photograph on a Sunday afternoon at Mud Lake Camp. Note the slab wood fuel piled in the tender of the locomotive. — FRANK KING COLLECTION

Paine & Company's *Chip*, shown at the center left, was the first locomotive on Minnesota's first logging railroad. Of unknown origin, she had seen some 30 years of service before coming to Carlton. — GEORGE B. ABDILL COLLECTION (BELOW) A rare view of the Paine Company sawmill at Carlton. Note the little saddle-tank locomotive at the right, which is almost obscured by smoke. This engine is believed to have been one of the first four engines constructed for the Northern Pacific and was identical to the famed *Minnetonka*. — CARLTON COUNTY HISTORICAL SOCIETY

19

Narrow-gauge Shay No. 7 was photographed with a log train on Mitchell Brother's Jennings & Northeastern Railroad en route to the mill at Jennings, Michigan. This Shay was built in 1896 and saw years of service in Virginia and West Virginia. — C. T. STONER COLLECTION

Rhapsody on Logging Railroads," the trade journal *Timberman* extolled the virtues of this modern improvement:

> In these modern days of extensive lumber operations, a lumberman's outfit is incomplete without a logging railroad; and the removal of a logging railway from one locality where the pine is exhausted to another yet uninvaded, excites no more comment than the removal of the camp and balance of the outfit of a heavy operator. These roads are too valuable usually to be abandoned; and the iron and rolling stock having become practically useless and valueless after having accomplished the purpose for which they were originally intended, are transferred to new locations where pine is plentiful. In several instances these logging railroads have been made the basis of a permanent line of road, and have served to develop the agricultural and other resources of the country through which they passed, and being extended have formed the connecting links between two main lines of road; and thriving villages along their lines have sprung into existence. The logging railroad has frequently been the pioneer in the civilization process of new and enterprising sections of the country, through the territory of which they forced their way somewhat after the fashion of an evangelist, when nothing apparently invited them except the stalwart forms of the monstrous pine trees, the branches of which swayed to and fro, exciting the enterprising tendencies of the lumbermen in the distance, who coveted the money value of nature's handiwork embraced in the massive forms, the development of which required centuries of time. Great is the logging railroad, and great is the business which is the incentive for planting them in the pineries. Who can conceive the possibilities embraced in a logging railway as it winds its tortuous way through the undeveloped regions, leaving immigration to follow in its wake. Some portions of the Huron Shore in Michigan owe their present prosperity and facilities for ingress and egress to the advent of the logging railroad; and several of the permanent roads branching out from the main lines of the Michigan Central and Flint & Pere Marquette roads, owe their existence to the logging railway which was built with no idea of permanence, but simply to secure the pine which was the basis of their existence.

The transportation cost advantage of the logging railroad was also recognized early by lumbermen. During 1889, the *Mississippi Valley Lumbermen* published a cost comparison based on a five-mile log haul by narrow-gauge railroad and by horse transportation. It showed that such a logging railroad would be able to handle 10 million board feet of logs in a 90-day season at a cost of 40 cents per thousand board feet, or one-tenth that of hauling the same quantity by horse teams.

By the early 1900's, the superiority of the logging railroad had become the "new gospel" for Minnesota loggers. The following newspaper account of the subject appeared in the *Duluth News Tribune* for November 17, 1901:

LOGGING ROADS BUILDING IN ALL DIRECTIONS . . . Twelve or fifteen years ago the lumbermen of northern Minnesota would have smiled broadly if anyone had predicted that in 1901, or before, more than half of the logging would be done by railroad and the system pronounced "the only way," as a prominent lumberman expressed it yesterday. Fifteen years ago it was figured that timber very far from water courses navigable for logs, was of comparatively little value as the only way it could be gotten out was by railroad, and this would be so expensive that there would be little or no profit in the transaction. Now rivers are a secondary consideration. They are taken advantage of if they are handy, but in many cases the logs are handled by rail in preference to the river where both water and rail are available. Instead of making the lumber business unprofitable to get logs out by rail, it has developed that there are greater profits in the business today than there were much of the time when river driving was the only means recognized for getting the logs to the mills. A logging road ten miles in length ten years ago was quite an institution, while now 25 to 75 miles excites no surprise.

Eventually, Minnesota's logging railroads ranged in size from the tiny J.M. Paine operation at Carlton to common carrier roads (offering their services to all comers for intra or interstate transportation) with as much as 100 miles of main line trackage. A good example of the latter was Alger-Smith Lumber Company's Duluth & Northern Minnesota Railway. The Duluth & Northern Minnesota was in many respects the most impressive and colorful logging railroad in Minnesota, and during its 20-year life span operated — in addition to its 100 miles of main line — a total of over 350 miles of branches and spurs.

Additional common carrier logging railroads included the 90-mile Brainerd & Northern Minnesota, now part of the Burlington Northern; Swan River Logging Company's Duluth, Mississippi River & Northern, which became part of the Great Northern; Itasca Lumber Company's 98-mile Minneapolis & Rainy River; and the Duluth & Northeastern, a one-time Weyerhaeuser affiliate which still operates a fraction of its former length.

Many logging railroads had no physical connection at all with other railroads in the area. Examples of these were the rail lines operated by the Estate of

A logging railroad loading scene in the forest primeval near Duluth during the 1890's. The link n' pin equipped flat cars shown here are owned by the ore-carrying Duluth, Missabe & Northern. — PETE BONESTEEL COLLECTION.

21

With white flags flying, D&IR Consolidation No. 46 pauses at Endion Station in Duluth with her train of logs bound for West Duluth sawmills. This interesting station has recently been placed on the National Historic Register. — FRANK KING COLLECTION

Thomas Nestor and the Split Rock Lumber Company, which extended back from Lake Superior into timberlands located along the Gooseberry and Split Rock River watersheds. Nestor's logs were rafted across Lake Superior to mills at Ashland, Wisconsin, and Baraga, Michigan, while Split Rock's were rafted to the mill operated by parent company Merrill & Ring at Duluth. The Lutsen Lumber Tie & Post Company operated a four-mile railroad between a vessel-loading dock on Lake Superior at Lockport and its inland sawmill on the Poplar River. This line, a lumber carrier rather than a logging railroad, operated between 1910 and 1912. Its motive power consisted of a sole Heisler-geared locomotive which, after the operation was abandoned, stood for almost 20 years forsaken on the shore of Lake Superior. Another isolated operation was St. Anthony Lumber Company's Northern Mississippi Railroad, which hauled logs to Cross Lake, from where they were floated to the Mississippi for movement to mills downstream.

A unique and isolated logging railroad operation was the portage road, which handled logs portage fashion between inland lakes. Swallow & Hopkins Lumber Company's four-mile logging railroad portage between Basswood and Fall lakes near Winton was a remarkable example. During its existence, over 300 million board feet of logs were handled by

23

the company's two wood-burning locomotives, in conjunction with a fleet of steam-powered tugs and launches which towed the logs in large booms across the two lakes. Other portage railroads in the same general area belonged to the Tower Lumber Company and the Trout Lake Lumber Company. Both of these operations were located at Lake Vermilion.

In addition to lines owned and operated by the various logging and lumber companies, there were many miles of logging spurs owned and operated by non-lumber-affiliated common carrier railroads in the area, e.g., the Duluth & Iron Range and the Duluth, Missabe & Northern, now part of the Duluth, Missabe & Iron Range. Each of these operated many miles of spur tracks devoted exclusively to logging.

Lumbering in northern Minnesota reached its peak at the turn of the century. During the winter months, the railroads were moving more than 3 million board feet of logs daily into the city of Duluth. The listing of board feet of logs handled in that area

A D&IR log train negotiates roller-coaster like trackage on a logging spur somewhere north of Two Harbors shortly after the turn of the century. — FRANK KING COLLECTION

During the early years of this century, the D&IR moved more logs into Duluth than any other railroad serving the city. In this view taken around 1910, No. 69, a big Schenectady-built 4-8-0 heads a log train near West Duluth. — FRANK KING COLLECTION

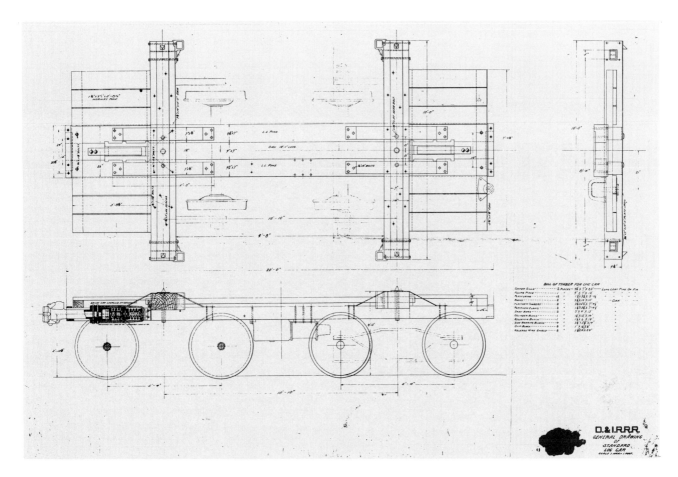

General drawing of a Duluth & Iron Range 20-foot log car. These cars were equipped with Bryan Car Coupling Attachments which were novel in the late 1890's. — FRANK KING COLLECTION

in 1901, either entirely or in part by rail, reads as follows:

Alger-Smith	100,000,000
Brooks-Scanlon	100,000,000
Duluth & Iron Range Railroad*	75,000,000
Duluth, Missabe & Northern Railway	50,000,000
Eastern Minnesota Railway	40,000,000
Swan River Logging Company	120,000,000
Powers and Simpson	65,000,000
Estate of Thomas Nestor	60,000,000
Split Rock Lumber Company	60,000,000
Tower Lumber Company	75,000,000
Duluth & Northeastern Railroad	60,000,000
Itasca Lumber Company	70,000,000

*Because of heavy ore traffic over its line into Two Harbors, the Duluth & Iron Range at this time embargoed all log movement north of that point from May 1 to November 1.

Including other logging railroad operations within the state, the total rail haulage of logs in Minnesota that year exceeded 1 billion board feet.

Minnesota's greatest all-time sawmilling center was Minneapolis, whose mills peaked at just under 600 million board feet in 1899. During the early 1880's, sawmills on the Duluth-Superior waterfront produced less than 5 million board feet annually. In 1902, a peak production of over 440 million board feet of white pine lumber was attained at the head of the lakes, a figure that exceeded Michigan's entire white pine lumber production for that year. By 1915, production had fallen below 100 million board feet, however, and Duluth's last sawmill closed in 1925. Between 1891 and 1924, more than 7 billion board feet of lumber were shipped to eastern and midwestern markets out of the Duluth-Superior harbor alone.

Minnesota's logging railroads reached their peak mileage around 1910. By that time, there were six common carrier railroads owned by lumber companies operating close to 400 main line miles, plus an estimated 200 miles of ever-changing branches and spurs. In addition, there were almost as many miles of logging railroads which never reached common carrier status. That year, the *American Lumberman* estimated the existence in the United States of some 2,000 logging railroads operating over 30,000 miles of track.

25

Log sorting works on the Mississippi River at Minneapolis, Minnesota, during the 1890's. Minneapolis was the world's greatest sawmilling center at the time. — MINNESOTA HISTORICAL SOCIETY

Lumbermen's axes made swift work of Minnesota's vast pine stands, and within another decade most of the logging railroads were gone. In 1921, the most colorful of them all, the Duluth & Northern Minnesota, received permission to abandon its remaining 99-mile main line.

The Virginia & Rainy Lake Company, operator of the largest white pine sawmill in the world, at Virginia on the famed Mesabi iron range, cut its last log in October 1929 after 20 years of operation. This giant mill, capable of turning out 1 million board feet of lumber a day when working two shifts of ten hours each, had an annual production capability of over 300 million board feet of lumber and related products. Its operation required the transportation services provided by some 140 miles of main line railroad equipped with 14 locomotives and some 350 log cars.

The Virginia & Rainy Lake Company had originally been conceived by Edward Hines as a merger of the remaining large Minnesota timber properties north of Virginia. Capitalized at $10,700,000, its stock was held by Hines, the Weyerhaeusers, and Cook & O'Brien, each owning about a one-third interest. The old Cook & O'Brien mill at Virginia formed the nucleus of the new complex, which became an unwieldy but impressively gigantic operation that attacked the pine forest to the north. In the end, however, the Virginia & Rainy Lake enterprise proved a disappointment and its owners barely recovered their investment.

By 1932, most of Minnesota's big saw timber had disappeared — her immense forests having produced a staggering total of over 67.5 billion board feet of lumber over the "roaring years." It was clear that a fabulous era in lumbering history was drawing to a close. In 1937, Minnesota's only remaining big sawmill, belonging to E.W. Backus' International Lumber Company at International Falls, cut its last log and wrote finis to a great industry.

This record double tier carload of 26 white pine logs contained some 16,200 board feet of timber. The average load for a 20-foot standard gauge Russel log car was only 5,000 board feet. — MINNESOTA HISTORICAL SOCIETY

26

This 1890 vintage advertisement from a logging trade journal offered Skeleton type logging cars weighting only 10,000 pounds each, but were capable of carrying a 60,000-pound load. — FRANK KING COLLECTION

Abandoned logging railroad trestle located on the Mile 48 Branch of the Duluth & Northern Minnesota Railway. — JOHN HOENE COLLECTION

One by one, the logging railroads, too, passed on into history. The Itasca Lumber Company's colorful Minneapolis & Rainy River Railway, locally known as the "Gut and Liver Route," somehow managed to keep going until the Depression, finally called it quits in 1932. By 1938, only slightly more than 300 miles of true logging railroads remained in the state. This total included 78 miles of International Lumber Company lines, 196 miles of General Logging Company lines, and 33 miles of White Cedar Timber Company lines. Of the common carrier logging railroads, only two survived: the Minneapolis, Red Lake & Manitoba; and the Duluth & Northeastern. During 1938, the former abandoned its lines, leaving only the Duluth & Northeastern. By then, most of the timber along the General Logging Company line, which connected with the end of the Duluth & Northeastern at Hornby, had been cut and those rails were taken up, severing the longest railroad log haul in Minnesota, which had extended from a point close to the Canadian border to Cloquet, a distance of nearly 200 miles. After that, there was little reason for the Duluth & Northeastern to maintain its Saginaw to Hornby line, and in 1941 permission was received to abandon the 46 miles of track between those two points, leaving only 11.4 miles of road between Saginaw on the Duluth, Missabe & Iron Range and Cloquet.

A clear picture of the relationship of log hauling by rail to over-all logging operations is basic to an understanding of the development of Minnesota's logging railroads. Thus, although the primary purpose of this volume, as indicated above, is to call long overdue attention to the roads themselves, the following chapters do contain at least brief descriptions of logging methods, camp life and conditions, and procedures and equipment used in cutting, log loading, and sawmilling.

2

THE LOGGING CAMP

The logging railroads changed logging camp lifestyles. The small camps prevalent in pre-railroad times increased in size and came to employ not 75 to 100 workers, but closer to 300 men. The periods of isolation that had been associated with camp life came to an end, rendering the long cold Minnesota winters more liveable for lumberjacks. Along with the railroads, came installation of camp telephones. At mealtimes, fresh meats and produce were no longer novelties, and returning to civilization was as simple as boarding the first train headed for town.

During the first decade of this century, the typical large logging camp operation consisted of two or three bunk-houses, a combined office and commissary, a kitchen and dining room, blacksmith's shop, saw filer's shack, horse barns, and a few other miscellaneous structures. Log buildings, used from the earliest days of logging, gave way to quickly-constructed lumber and tarpaper ones. The life span of the average camp varied from one to two years, and at its end windows, doors, and frames were removed to be used again at another location. By 1920, electric lighting in the woods was no longer uncommon.

The food in the camps, while not "fancy," was usually good and plentiful. Indeed, the success of a logging camp depended largely upon the quality of its cuisine. Word of a mediocre table circulated quickly.

Interestingly enough, some of the better cooks during the final days of Minnesota logging worked on the iron ore boats that plied the Great Lakes in summer, and switched to the camps in winter. Their return was eagerly anticipated by the railroad men, most of whom considered themselves critical epicureans. Throughout any day, a big pot of coffee would always be brewing on the back of the cookstove for foremen, scalers, railroad men, cruisers, and clerks who stopped by for a cup or two. For between meal snacks, the cook also kept on hand an ample supply of fresh doughnuts, pie, and cake.

The professional American logger, better known as the "lumberjack," can trace his ancestry to the once vast forests of Maine in the years before the signing of the Declaration of Independence. Joined by other woodsmen from New England and by men from Canada and Europe, the lumberjacks cut their way west into the Lake States, as well as into the South, and eventually moved to the giant timber stands in the Pacific Northwest.

Although logging itself was conducive to a healthy existence, life within the early lumber camp was not always pleasant. Overcrowded and crudely furnished bunkhouses and strong odors of perspiration, tobacco smoke, and wet clothing combined to create an unusual atmosphere. Many early camps

An 1880's logging camp scene near Rhinelander, Wisconsin. Logger Alfred Greenwood, the third from the left, was the maternal grandfather of the author. He owned and operated this and other camps in Michigan and Wisconsin. (BELOW LEFT) Lumberjacks gather around the camp stove before going to their evening meal. (BELOW) The head cook, shown in the center, was usually the highest paid man in camp. — FRANK KING COLLECTION

One of the loggers performed the task of camp barber on Sundays. (FAR RIGHT) The kitchen staff pose proudly with their freshly baked bread and pastries. Note flour barrels below the counter. — BOTH FRANK KING COLLECTION

Sunday in camp was usually spent in relaxing and the washing of clothes. — FRANK KING COLLECTION

The larger camps employed a saw filer to keep all saws in shape. This photograph was taken at Kileen & Company camp in 1914. — FRANK KING COLLECTION

Their days work done, lumberjacks relax in front of their bunks before turning in for the night. Note the clothing and footware hanging up to dry. — FRANK KING COLLECTION

The blacksmith was a key man in the logging camp. He was called upon to perform everything from shoeing horses to making repair parts for logging equipment ranging from sleighs to logging cars. These men are at work at Colbroth Camp No. 4 near Duluth in 1912. —FRANK KING COLLECTION

31

Sawyers working for Brooks-Scanlon cut a fallen tree to the desired lengths before loading on rail cars. Standard log lengths were 12, 14, 16 and 18 feet, depending upon the tree and mill requirements, with 16 feet being the most common length. (RIGHT) Alger-Smith sawyers about to cut up a fallen monarch of the forest. The men could usually cut up about 100 white pine logs in a given day. — FRANK KING COLLECTION

An Alger-Smith team skids a log to the nearest rail spur. Skidding was usually restricted to about 40 rods. — FRANK KING COLLECTION

A St. Croix Six team of gray horses hauls in camp supplies for the St. Croix Lumber & Manufacturing Company near Winton, Minnesota. — FRANK KING COLLECTION

contained beds of pine boughs, only later replaced by straw mattresses. Either style of bed made an excellent home for vermin and rodents. It was not until World War I days that logging camps provided their residents with such amenities as showers with running water, bed sheets, laundry equipment, and electric lighting.

Lumberjacks' wages, in general, were comparable to those of farm workers or cowhands. Significantly, the cook for a large crew was usually the highest-paid man in the camp. The October 1, 1930 International Lumber Company wage schedule for woodsmen is reproduced below:

INTERNATIONAL LUMBER COMPANY
Wage Schedule for Woodsmen
October 1 - 1930

	Per Month
General Work	$20.00
Swampers	20.00
Tailing Down (Considered General Work)	20.00
Skidding Teamsters	26.00
Cross Haul Teamsters	26.00
Sawyers	26.00
Handymen	40.00
Loaders	26.00
Two Horse Teamsters (Sleigh Haul)	26.00
Four Horse Teamsters (Sleigh Haul)	$40.00 to 45.00
Six Horse Teamsters (Sleigh Haul)	40.00 to 45.00
Saw Filers	40.00
Four Horse Tote Teamsters	30.00
Section Boss	50.00
Section Men	20.00
Steel Gang Men	35.00
Engineer Steam Jammer	80.00
Top Loader Steam Jammer	50.00
Top Loader's Helper Steam Jammer	40.00
Bull Cook Steam Jammer	35.00
Hooker Steam Jammer	35.00
Buncher Steam Jammer	30.00
Pincher Steam Jammer	30.00
Top Loader Sleigh Haul	35.00
Hooker Sleigh Haul	30.00
Hook Men Tailing Down on Sleigh Haul	26.00
Landing Men Sleigh Haul	26.00
Road Monkey	20.00

	Per Calendar Month
Straw Boss	50.00
Saw Boss	45.00
Barn Boss	35.00
Blacksmith	70.00 to 75.00
Cook, Small Crew	60.00 to 80.00
Cook, Large Crew	90.00
Second Cook	45.00
Cookee	30.00
Bull Cook	30.00
Jammer Watchman	30.00
Locomotive Watchman	45.00
Night Watchman Around Camp	20.00

The one fringe benefit the lumberjack enjoyed, unmatched in any other occupation, was good food and plenty of it. Approximately five pounds of provisions were required each day to feed one working logger.

The average lumberjack has often been sterotyped as a rough or crude sort. This assessment is in many respects misleading and incorrect. Contrary to popular opinion, not all lumberjacks "blew their stakes" each spring. Many a man saved his earnings and supported a wife and children at home. Some loggers were men with excellent educations, who found life in the woods a way to evade the cares and problems of the world. That they did their job and did it well cannot be denied. Untold thousands of decaying pine stumps provide mute testimony to their strenuous efforts in a bygone era.

Lumberjacks pause during the noon hour for a hot lunch in the woods at Fortin's camp near Ridge. — FRANK KING COLLECTION

33

It was a cold winter day when Brainerd & Northern Minnesota Railway No. 3 paused for the wet plate camera while en route to Brainerd with a load of fresh cut timber. — GERALD M. BEST COLLECTION

3

THE RIVER RAILROADS

Minnesota's first logging railroads, by connecting the pineries with the upper Mississippi and St. Croix rivers, provided a low-cost means of transportation for the remainder of the distance to the mills. Sawmills were located at Brainerd, Little Falls, Minneapolis, Winona, and — in some cases — at river towns far to the south in Iowa and Illinois. Among the more important railroads were those operated by the Itasca Lumber Company; Wright, Davis & Company; and the Minnesota Logging Company.

In 1887, W.T. Joyce of Clinton, Iowa, joined Minneapolis lumberman H.C. Akeley in establishing the Itasca Lumber Company. In 1890, their firm began construction of a logging railroad, incorporated as the Itasca Railroad (and sometimes called the Bass Brook Railroad) from Itasca on the Mississippi (now known as Cohasset) into the timberlands. From the landing, where logs were dumped for driving downstream to mills at Minneapolis and in Iowa, its rails extended north some 18 miles into the pine forests. Records indicate that the little Itasca Railroad had only one locomotive, a diamond-stacked Porter-built Mogul, in operation from 1891 until 1898, when a second engine, also of the Mogul type, arrived from the Brooks Locomotive Works.

The Itasca Railroad continued to operate from Cohasset until 1897, at which time the steel rails

were removed and sent to Deer River, then a frontier town located a few miles north at the end of the Duluth & Winnipeg Railway. It seems that J.P. Sims, then general manager of the Itasca Lumber Company, was unable to negotiate what he considered to be a reasonable price for additional lands along the Mississippi and ordered his crews to pick up the rails. On August 1, 1901, the property of the Itasca Railroad was purchased by the Minneapolis & Rainy River Railway, also owned by the Itasca Lumber Company. The Minneapolis & Rainy River had been incorporated in perpetuity only a few days before — on July 20, to be exact. F.C. Gerhard, who represented the Joyce interests, became general manager of both the lumber company and the railway, and he was responsible for extension of the line to its ultimate length.

Motive power on the Itasca Railroad in 1901 totaled four locomotives — three Moguls and one American. In 1911, the Minneapolis & Rainy River had 11 locomotives on the roster, averaging 47 tons in weight and slightly over 17,000 pounds tractive effort. Rolling stock consisted of 272 log cars, 92 flatcars, 8 boxcars, 4 passenger cars, and 4 miscellaneous cars. As early as 1914, the road had a surplus of equipment, and 50 logging cars were sold that year to the Hume-Bennett Lumber Company in California's

The woodburning locomotive *Itasca* spots cars for loading on the Itasca Railroad. Logs are being loaded in this scene by the tripod method. Here logs are brought up to the tripod in an orderly manner by means of a pond-like trench.
—MINNESOTA HISTORICAL SOCIETY

Looking north along the Minneapolis & Rainy River main line from White Oak Lake, a widening of the Mississippi River. The sawmill on the left, owned by parent Itasca Lumber Company, consumed only a portion of the logs dumped here, the bulk being floated down river to mills at Minneapolis and beyond. (RIGHT) M&RR logging train pauses on a trestle over the Big Fork River to syphon water into the tender. — BOTH FRANK KING COLLECTION

Log rollway at Deer River stretched for nearly a mile on the ice of White Oak Lake. This was along the dump trestle of the Minneapolis & Rainy River Railroad. — FRANK KING COLLECTION

The Dickson Manufacturing Co. built No. 7 which was a favorite on the *Gut and Liver Route*, the nickname of the Minneapolis & Rainy River. (LEFT) The M&RR and parent Itasca Lumber Company shared this combined office and depot at Deer River. The small sign on the corner of the building announced that men were wanted for employment by the Deer River Lumber Company. — FRANK KING COLLECTION

Minneapolis & Rainy River No. 10 with crew. (LEFT) The road's homemade inspection car on the turntable at their Deer River roundhouse. — FRANK KING COLLECTION

Mishap at the Minneapolis & Rainy River-Great Northern crossing at Deer River. The view above shows M&RR No. 5 after being struck by Great Northern No. 1594 which was backing up to pick up its train following the taking of water. The GN's "big hook" was called from Superior, Wisconsin to place old No. 5 back on the rails as is shown at the left. Five's frame was so badly bent in the mishap, even with subsequent efforts to straighten it, she was never the same. — BOTH FRANK KING COLLECTION

Grading crew pushing construction of the Minneapolis & Rainy River through Big Fork during 1905. Before the coming of mechanical graders and tractors, this was the way a right-of-way was leveled before the placing of ties and the spiking down of rails. — MINNESOTA HISTORICAL SOCIETY

A 1912 vintage train of the M&RR poses on the trestle over Big Fork River. Note the unique star-shaped number plate on the smokebox of No. 5. The combine at the end of the train accommodated those who paid first class fares, while the crude coach was reserved for lumberjacks. (LEFT) M&RR No. 8 with a log train. Note the logs slipping off the first log flat in the train.
—BOTH FRANK KING COLLECTION

Train time at Big Fork station on the Minneapolis & Rainy River. The structure exhibits austere architecture lines. PETE BONESTEEL COLLECTION (LEFT) The crew of an M&RR mixed train pose with their waycar at some long forgotten location along the line. — FRANK KING COLLECTION

A four car Great Northern passenger train from Duluth is about to cross the M&RR rails at Deer River, circa 1910. A M&RR box car, located on an interchange track, may be seen in the lower right hand corner of the above scene. — LEE BROWNELL COLLECTION (RIGHT) M&RR 4-4-0 No. 12 awaits orders at Deer River station before heading up the line. — PETE BONESTEEL COLLECTION (BELOW) Engine No. 12 was the last locomotive over the road. She is shown here backing down the line with the rail scrapping train late in 1932. — HAROLD VAN HORN COLLECTION

Employees Time Table No. 10 of the Minneapolis & Rainy River Railway dated February 11, 1918. The road operated two trains daily between Deer River and Alder, with one running to Craig, 41 miles down the line; the other to Stanley, a distance of 36 miles. — WAYNE C. OLSON COLLECTION

redwood country. By 1924, equipment ownership had shrunk to 5 locomotives, 67 flatcars, 4 passenger cars, and 14 miscellaneous cars. By then, all the logging cars were gone, reflecting the drastic decline in logging activities.

The Minneapolis & Rainy River's general offices, shops, and roundhouse were at Deer River. Although the road was usually called "the M&R," old-timers liked to call it the "Gut & Liver Route," a reference to the preponderance of liver sausage in the cuisine of the logging camps along the line.

By 1907, total trackage was 52.72 miles. Tracks extended from the landing at White Oak Lake on the Mississippi to Big Fork, 31.69 miles; Marcell Junction to Marcell, 1.59 miles; Jessie Junction to Bass Lake, 17.84 miles; and Whitefish Junction to Whitefish, 1.60 miles. Peak mileage of 97.86, of which 33.07 miles were owned outright by the parent Itasca Lumber Company, was attained in 1911. Tracks were laid with 56-, 60-, and 65-pound rails.

During 1931, with the Depression under way, gross revenues on the Minneapolis & Rainy River dipped to just under $40,000, resulting in a deficit of $26,000 for the year. In early 1932, trying to reduce operating losses, the company petitioned the Minnesota Railroad and Warehouse Commission for permission to cease operation of daily mixed train service and asked to be allowed to operate trains on an "as needed" basis.

After due consideration of all matters involved, the Commission ruled:

That the present train service could not be entirely abandoned without substantial injury to the public but that, under the present general period of depression, the present daily service could be curtailed and a properly scheduled tri-weekly service would under present existing conditions, reasonably serve the public, and no substantial injury would result therefrom to the public.

Accordingly, tri-weekly train service went into effect on March 1, 1932. As the company had predicted, however, this reduction in service proved insufficient to curb mounting operating losses. Application for abandonment was filed, and it was granted on August 27, 1932. Shortly thereafter, the rails were picked up, and the remaining three locomotives and 74 cars were sent to Duluth for scrapping.

Log loading on the Duluth, Mississippi River & Northern using the cross-haul method. A team of horses on the opposite side of the car provide the power to move the logs aboard the car. Note the tender on Porter-built Mogul No. 2 which was equipped with a pilot and back-up headlight. — FRANK KING COLLECTION

Grading the Duluth & Winnipeg Railroad west of Grand Rapids in 1890. The Wright & Davis logging interests were active in pushing construction of the road in order to obtain a connection at Swan River for their logging railroad, the Duluth, Mississippi River & Northern. The D&W, thwarted in its attempt to reach Winnipeg, was acquired by the Great Northern in 1898 and to this day carries heavy tonnages of ore and grain to the Head of the Lakes. — ITASCA COUNTY HISTORICAL SOCIETY

Down river a few miles from the Itasca Lumber Company's operations, the Saginaw, Michigan logging firm of Wright, Davis & Company in 1891 began construction of a similar logging railroad. This line, chartered as the Duluth, Mississippi River & Northern, extended northward from Mississippi Landing at the mouth of the Swan River on the Mississippi. Construction progressed steadily, and in 1895 reached the booming iron mining town of Hibbing. Timber which would normally have gone down the St. Louis River to mills at Cloquet, only 50 miles south, was floated via the Mississippi 150 miles south to Minneapolis — or as far as 500 miles to long-established mills in Iowa and Illinois. The Duluth, Mississippi River & Northern was a busy road, consistently hauling to the Mississippi about 100 million board feet of logs per year.

The February 1895 *Mississippi Valley Lumberman* contained an excellent description of the log landing on the Mississippi, in which the author mentioned seeing more logs assembled there than had ever been seen collected in any rollway up to that time:

> There were over 45,000,000 feet on the rollway, and the logs extended in a magnificent stretch for a mile down the stream, until lost to view by a bend in the Mississippi. They were piled nearly the full width of the stream, and were 25 to 30 tiers deep, reaching from the bottom of the river to the level of the tracks. The sight was an impressive one, and long to be remembered.

An even greater sight to lumbermen was the 75 million board feet of pine assembled at the Brainerd

Brooks-built Mogul No. 8 heads a logging train on the Duluth, Mississippi River & Northern Railroad, circa 1899. — MINNESOTA HISTORICAL SOCIETY

An official eyes the derailment of Mogul No. 8 and the destruction of several empty Russel log cars on the Duluth, Mississippi River & Northern. — ITASCA HISTORICAL SOCIETY (BELOW) Loading logs onto Russel cars on the DMR&N during the 1890's using a homemade slide jammer. — GARRIE L. TUFFORD COLLECTION

Duluth, Mississippi River & Northern No. 4 emerges from the pine forests pulling a train stacked high with logs sometime during 1894. The road was acquired by James J. Hill for his Great Northern in 1899 and his Brooks-built Mogul eventually wound up on a logging railroad in Missouri —

FRANK KING COLLECTION

landing of the Brainerd & Northern Minnesota Railway on the Mississippi one year later. Within the logging industry, such records were only made to be broken!

By 1898, motive power on the Duluth, Mississippi River & Northern consisted of nine locomotives, all but one of them of the Mogul type. The exception was engine No. 9, a Ten-Wheeler received that year. Aside from the first two locomotives, which came from Porter, all motive power was acquired new from the Brooks Locomotive Works. This was rather unusual, as most Minnesota logging railroads were content to make do with a motive power fleet of secondhand locomotives acquired from trunk lines or other logging companies.

During 1897, rails were laid eastward from Hibbing to Chisholm, and in 1898 extended north to the main logging operations around Dewey Lake. In 1899, the affiliated Swan River Logging Company Limited constructed 15 miles of line eastward from Hibbing across the Mesabi Range into Virginia. (Both the Swan River Logging Company Limited and the Duluth, Mississippi River & Northern were acquired that year by James J. Hill and, as a result, the line between Hibbing and Virginia was actually built for his account.) This trackage was subsequently acquired by the Great Northern through its Eastern Railway of Minnesota in 1902.

In 1895, once its tracks had reached Hibbing, the Duluth, Mississippi River & Northern entered into a traffic contract with the Duluth & Winnipeg Railway to handle ore from the newly-opened Mahoning Mine near Hibbing to a connection with the latter's road at Swan River. That year, the road handled some 250,000 tons of ore, in addition to 75 million board feet of pine. Shortly afterwards, James J. Hill acquired the Duluth & Winnipeg in line with his general scheme of extending his Great Northern Railway westward from Duluth. By connecting with existing lines at or near Crookston, Minnesota, Hill provided a direct rail outlet for grain moving from the Dakotas to the head of Lake Superior.

For some time, D.M. Philbin, general superintendent of the Duluth & Winnipeg, at the urging of the Merritt Brothers (famed discoverers of the Mesabi), had been taking every opportunity to persuade Hill to acquire the cut-over Wright, Davis & Company property which included some 25,000 acres of unexplored land on the Mesabi Range. Philbin, who came from the recently constructed Duluth, Missabe & Northern, of which he had been general manager, felt strongly that this was property of great value. Hill became convinced. Purchase of the entire property was completed, and on May 1, 1899 the papers were signed. For this, including the logging railroad and the lands, Hill paid $4,050,000. Much of the land was cut over, some was under stumpage

One of many log rollways along the Duluth, Mississippi River & Northern. Teams of horses, like those shown in the distance, helped pile the logs to such heights. — GARRIE L. TUFFORD COLLECTION

Swan River station, located at the junction of the Duluth, Mississippi River & Northern and the Duluth & Winnipeg roads, was a busy transfer point during the 1890's for passengers bound for the logging camps and the booming mining community of Hibbing. — JOHN H. HEARDING COLLECTION (BELOW) A DMR&N trip pass issued in 1898 for a one way trip between Hibbing and Swan River. — FRANK KING COLLECTION

45

Great Northern Mogul No. 357 pauses at Swan River in the early 1900's with an ancient combination car-caboose before heading north up the former DRM&N road to Hibbing. This run had been named the "Wooden Shoe" by the early loggers because of the rough riding characteristics of the track and equipment. This moniker remained with the train long after the logging days were but a memory. — WAYNE C. OLSEN COLLECTION

contract, and some was known or assumed to contain minerals.

Even at take-over time, the heavy grades encountered on the former logging road proved a serious limitation to the efficient handling of ore tonnage over the line. To improve the situation, Great Northern chief engineer J.F. Stevens authorized a preliminary survey during the summer of 1899. The prime objective was to ascertain the practicability of reducing grades as opposed to building a new road. Grade reduction was selected as the more immediate economical solution. Leighton, Beauty Lake, Gardner, and Pan Cake Hills were subsequently cut down from one percent to six-tenths of one percent grade against the eastbound loaded movement. By 1900, ore traffic had become so heavy that the Great Northern constructed a new line some 30 miles to the east, with a ruling grade of less than three-tenths of one percent. From then on, the Swan River line was used almost exclusively for the westbound empty movement.

During 1960, as a result of installation of Centralized Traffic Control (CTC) on portions of its Mesabi Division, the Great Northern made various operational changes. The one-time logging railroad, still being used only for westbound empty ore trains, was by then no longer required, and the trackage between Swan River and Kelly Lake was removed. The portion of the old line between Swan River and Mississippi Landing had been removed a quarter century earlier, when the Hill City Railway ceased operation over its 17.5-mile line. This road, which was organized in 1915, upon acquisition of the entire property of the Mississippi, Hill City & Western Railway, served Armour's National Woodenware plant at Hill City and enjoyed trackage rights over six miles of the Great Northern into Swan River.

Once the Duluth, Mississippi River & Northern became part of the Great Northern system, it was merged into the Northern — later the Mesabi — Division. The cut over Wright, Davis & Company lands soon revealed immense deposits of hundreds of millions of tons of rich iron. By 1906, the Great Northern was handling over 6 million tons of ore annually, and its line between Swan River and Superior, Wisconsin was soon double-tracked. Six years later, annual ore tonnage over the Great Northern alone reached nearly 14 million, and to this day the Mesabi Range remains the principal domestic source of iron ore.

Hill City Railway Consolidation No. 7 cannot deny her Pennsylvania Railroad origin. — HAROLD VAN HORN COLLECTION (RIGHT) No. 907, a brand new Rhode Island-built Ten Wheeler, prepares to depart the Mahoning Mine Yard near Hibbing with a special train carrying railway and mining dignitaries during the latter part of 1899. The train will travel over the former Wright & Davis logging railroad. — JOHN H. HEARDING COLLECTION

James J. Hill's acquisition of the cut over Wright & Davis timberlands on the Mesabi Range resulted in his Great Northern Railway becoming an important iron ore carrier by the turn of the century. This photograph taken on June 23, 1923, shows Great Northern Mallet No. 2022 at the head of a test train of 150 ore cars grossing 13,221 tons which would soon become standard ore train weight over the Mesabi Division. — BURLINGTON NORTHERN COLLECTION

Northern Mill Company's three wood-burning narrow-gauge locomotives pose for a portrait at Gilpatrick Lake landing during 1891. Little two-cylindered Shay No. 1, leading the trio, was likely acquired secondhand from a Michigan logging company. Shay No. 3, bringing up the rear, was purchased new in 1890. — CROW WING COUNTY HISTORICAL SOCIETY

An 1890 scene illustrating the log loading process on Northern Mill Company's narrow-gauge railway near Gull Lake. — MINNESOTA HISTORICAL SOCIETY

An interesting sidelight to this narrative dates back to 1891, when Wright and Davis placed some 45,000 acres of their timberlands up for sale for $1,200,000. The Weyerhaeuser group expressed interest; but a disagreement arose regarding the asking price. It seems that Davis firmly believed that his land contained iron ore, but refused to include the mineral rights in the sale unless presented with an additional $100,000. Frederick Weyerhaeuser was prepared to pay. His associates, however, were not convinced of the presence of iron and recommended taking only the timber rights. They were to regret that decision. A few years later, so the story goes, Weyerhaeuser, while watching a Great Northern train pass by containing ore mined from the Wright and Davis properties, turned to his companion — after counting some 50 cars — and remarked "and to think we could have had all of that for only $100,000!"

In 1880, prominent Minneapolis lumberman Charles A. Pillsbury formed the Gull River Lumber Company and built a sawmill at the Northern Pacific crossing of Gull River, about ten miles west of Brainerd. The company owned substantial tracts of timber along Gull River and Gull Lake. Logs cut along the shores of Gull Lake were formed into rafts, towed across the lake by steamboat to Gull River, and floated down river to the Gull River mill. Many logs were sent beyond, to mills at Minneapolis.

Log-cutting operations made swift work of the timber around Gull Lake, and to keep the mill in operation, the vast pine forests extending some 10 to 20 miles west were soon acquired. It became impossible to rely solely on water transportation for log

The log landing at Gilpatrick Lake doesn't appear to have room for any more logs, but a train of narrow-gauge log cars waits on the siding for unloading. — MINNESOTA HISTORICAL SOCIETY

movement, and in 1889 the company constructed an inland narrow-gauge (three-foot) railroad to tap the newly acquired timber. The unincorporated road was known as the Minnesota Logging Railroad, and its headquarters was located at Gilpatrick Lake. Logs were moved over the narrow-gauge road to the log dump at Gilpatrick Lake (now know as Lake Margaret) for rafting across Gull Lake and down Gull River to the mill. In marked contrast to Michigan and Wisconsin, this was Minnesota's only narrow-gauge logging railroad; however, this fact was consistent with the general national decline of narrow-gauge construction and operation as the turn of the century approached.

Late in 1889, the Minnesota Logging Railroad was incorporated as the Gull Lake & Northern Railway Company. The charter provided for building a logging railroad from Gull Lake to the northern border of the state. The December 6, 1889 issue of the *Mississippi Valley Lumberman* stated that the railroad, which was narrow-gauge, had been building for sometime, and that other loggers in the area, including the Backus, Shevlin, Scanlon, and Carpenter interests, also planned to make use of it to transport their logs.

By January 1890, narrow-gauge rails extended some 12 miles northwesterly from the landing at Gilpatrick Lake, and there were, in addition, six miles of spurs into the heavy pine areas. Some 55 million board feet of logs were handled over the railroad that winter. Motive power at the time consisted of a small secondhand Shay-geared locomotive for use on the spurs and a classic Baldwin Mogul for handling log trains over the main line. A third and final narrow-gauge locomotive, a new Lima-built

Shay, arrived during December 1890. The *Brainerd Dispatch* for December 19 reported:

We have been much interested in the progress made by the party moving a new engine into the woods for use on the (Minnesota Logging) lumber railroad. It has been en route by land and sea for about three weeks and hopes to reach port in time to hang up Christmas stockings.

The narrow-gauge did a thriving business throughout the 1890-91 and 1891-92 logging seasons. Main line trackage was extended into the Moose and Spider lake areas, and new spurs, to facilitate cutting of the large pine stands, reached out in all directions.

It had been foreseen by this time that all the pine remaining in the Gull Lake region would soon be cut over. The area surrounding Leech Lake, however, some 40 to 60 miles north of Brainerd, contained immense stands of timber. Due to its inaccessibility to streams large enough to float logs, this region was practically untouched.

Some six years earlier, a bill providing for construction of a dam across the Mississippi River at Brainerd had been submitted to Congress. The proposal called for a dam 20 feet in height that would be capable of generating some 25,000 horsepower and, in addition, would provide an excellent millpond. In 1888, financial assistance for the project was obtained from the village of Brainerd, and Charles Kindred began construction of the dam.

Four years later, the Northern Mill Company was formed. This company leased the Gull River Lumber Company and its narrow-gauge Gull Lake & Northern Railway and moved the Gull River sawmill to Brainerd. Moving timber from Leech Lake to Brainerd, however, necessitated rail transportation. Thus, on May 16, 1892, the Brainerd & Northern Minnesota Railway came into being. Its officers included such prominent Minnesota lumbermen as E.P. Welles, president and general manager; J.E. Carpenter, vice-president; W.F. Brooks, secretary; and E.L. Carpenter, treasurer. Financial assistance to construct the new line was solicited from the citizens of Brainerd and Crow Wing County, who overwhelmingly approved a $100,000 bond issue for the purpose.

Plans for the Brainerd & Northern Minnesota involved separating the railway into two divisions: the Southern Division, extending from Brainerd to Gilpatrick Lake; and the Northern Division, extending northwest from Gilpatrick Lake and incorporating Northern Mill's narrow-gauge railroad (the Gull Lake & Northern). Specifications for the new line called for 60-pound rail; however, in an effort to reduce construction costs, 45-pound rails were laid instead.

This towboat was used by Northern Mill Company to move logs across Gull Lake. This operation ceased when the Gull River mill was moved to Brainerd. — MINNESOTA HISTORICAL SOCIETY (BELOW) Northern Mill Company's Shay No. 3 with a narrow-gauge log train at Gilpatrick Lake. Note how the region is completely denuded of trees. — CROW WING COUNTY HISTORICAL SOCIETY

Brainerd & Northern Minnesota's Baldwin-built Mogul No. 2, the *James B. Ransom*, was named after the road's treasurer. She came to the road new in 1892. — H. L. BROADBELT COLLECTION

Construction of the Brainerd & Northern Minnesota out of Brainerd began in late July 1892 with over 40 miles of grading. By October, a 673-foot trestle across Gull Lake narrows was nearing completion. Conversion of the narrow-gauge to standard went ahead rapidly. On January 13, 1893, the Crow Wing County commissioners received an engineering report:

> ... (the Brainerd & Northern Minnesota Railway) ... has been widened to 4'8-½" uniform gauge and has taken up the old (narrow gauge) rails weighing 36 pounds ... and has laid in place new (45 pound) steel rails ... A telegraph line is nearly completed for the entire length (of the main line) of both divisions, a distance of 28 miles.

Brainerd & Northern Minnesota standard gauge equipment at the time consisted of two Baldwin 40-ton Moguls, three secondhand 22-ton Forney type engines (no reference to which is made in any subsequent rosters), one combination baggage-passenger car with seats for 28 passengers, and a large fleet of logging cars, most of them built by the Duluth Manufacturing Company. Log traffic over the standard gauge road began during January 1893, with four trains of 20 cars each operating daily into Brainerd.

The Northern Mill Company had standard gauged its line from Gilpatrick Lake to Spider Lake with the intention of incorporating this trackage into the northern extension of the Brainerd & Northern Minnesota to Leech Lake. However, during January 1893, a preliminary survey for a more direct route between Lake Hubert and Leech Lake was authorized — even though the northern terminus of the

A former New York Elevated Railway Forney-type (0-4-4) picks up loaded Russel cars on what is believed to be the Brainerd & Northern Minnesota. The little engine was among many of its type which found their way into the woods upon electrification of the elevated railroads. — DOUGLAS COUNTY HISTORICAL SOCIETY

Brainerd & Northern Minnesota Railway's No. 3 heads a log train south through Walker along the shore of Leech Lake during 1896. This wood-burning Mogul engine was built for the road only the year before this photograph was made. Note the painted No. 3 on the headlight lens. — MINNESOTA HISTORICAL SOCIETY

existing road was approximately 20 miles closer to Leech Lake than the point where the new extension would begin. The revised routing was intended to eliminate the heavy expense of building through the rather rough country between Spider and Leech lakes. Trackage from Lake Hubert to Spider Lake was removed during 1894, slightly more than one year after its conversion from narrow to standard gauge.

The term "narrow gauge" is applied to any railway whose gauge is less than the standard 4'8-½", and it is interesting to note the contrast between Michigan's and Minnesota's logging railroads in this regard. In 1885, Michigan had no fewer than 57 narrow-gauge railroads, reflecting a total of seven different track gauges ranging from 34-½" to 48". Two factors were primarily responsible for this: (1) Such railroads could be built and equipped for approximately one-half the cost of standard-gauge roads. (2) The lighter weight of narrow-gauge locomotives and rolling stock facilitated their transport over land or by water to location of use. The latter consideration was of great importance because many of Michigan's early logging railroads initially had no physical connection with established common carrier railway systems. In Minnesota, on the other hand, the desire of lumbermen to be able to interchange cars with established common carriers brought about (with the exception of the Gull Lake & Northern) adherence to standard gauge on that state's logging railroads. Many Minnesota loggers were veterans of Michigan logging operations, too, and vividly recalled the limitations imposed by narrow-gauge operations there.

The gigantic sale in March 1894 of 1.5 billion board feet of standing timber by the Walker, Akeley, and Pillsbury interests to a new concern known as the Minnesota Logging Company created great excitement within the logging industry. In June of that year, a contract was let to Foley Brothers & Gutherie to extend the Brainerd & Northern Minnesota from Hubert to Walker on the shore of Leech Lake, a distance of 42 miles. Construction of the road proceeded at a good pace, with the end of steel reaching Lothrup, 51 miles from Brainerd, by early 1895. The woods headquarters of the Minnesota Logging Company and the railway for advanced operations were located there.

In the meantime, however, the Brainerd & Northern Minnesota's railroad project had overtaxed the financial resources of the Northern Mill Company, which backed its construction, and in

November 1894 the Brainerd Lumber Company was formed to acquire the Northern Mill properties, which had lain idle through the summer due to depressed business conditions.

The *Mississippi Valley Lumberman*, in an 1895 issue featuring the Brainerd & Northern Minnesota, presented a colorful description of the up and coming town of Lothrop:

> There is a considerable town here for a starter. There is one well defined street, and two hotels are the largest buildings with the exception of the company's structures. The latter consists of a large warehouse where are stored the supplies necessary to the work of construction; a large boarding house where the force now employed, and consisting of one hundred men are fed; an office building; an engine house, with stalls for three engines and machine shops for car and tool repairing. Here at Lothrop is one of the prettiest lakes of the 20,000 (the state now prides itself on having 10,000) that are said to lie within the confines of the state.

Today, Lothrop has vanished completely.

The Brainerd & Northern Minnesota was also publicized in the *Railway Age* of September 27, 1895, which reported:

> The Brainerd & Northern Minnesota, the greatest logging railroad in the world, has this summer laid about 25 miles of branches and 15 miles of main line to the north end of Leech Lake.

That year, persistent rumors circulated that the road would become part of the Great Northern system, to be used as a link in its proposed Duluth to Fosston line (which would have passed through Brainerd and Mille Lacs).

By 1896, the Brainerd & Northern Minnesota was operating more than 60 miles of main line and 40 miles of temporary spurs, and boasted an electrically-lighted log landing on the Mississippi at Brainerd, quite an innovation for the time. Motive power consisted of ten locomotives of the Mogul type, and a fleet of some 500 logging cars kept logs moving from the woods to Brainerd. During the winter of 1895-96, heavy log traffic required the movement of four or five trains daily, each carrying 35 to 40 loads of logs. The 31.79-mile extension from Walker to Bemidji was completed on December 17, 1898. The following year, the road hauled 347,864 tons of freight and carried 25,546 passengers, with net earnings of $89,897.

The southern terminus of the Brainerd & Northern Minnesota was located near the Northern Mill in East Brainerd, approximately three miles from the Northern Pacific's Brainerd depot. Although the Brainerd & Northern Minnesota was physically connected to the Northern Pacific by means of a spur owned by the latter, no passenger service was provided over this line. To transport mill workers and Brainerd & Northern Minnesota passengers between Brainerd and East Brainerd, a three-mile trolley line was constructed in 1893 by the Brainerd Electric Street Railway.

The Great Hinckley Fire of 1894 destroyed vast stands of timber in north central Minnesota. As a result of the fire, many logging companies operating in the area were forced to change their plans in order to salvage damaged timber as quickly as possible. In this scene along the rails of the Brainerd & Northern Minnesota in 1895, the loading crew posed long enough for a bit of pugilistic clowning. — FRANK KING COLLECTION

During 1897, the electric street railway fell on hard times, and its officers decided not to rebuild the wind-damaged, quarter-mile-long timber trestle on their line to East Brainerd. Shortly after this, the trolley company went out of business. The Northern Pacific, perhaps wishing to block the Great Northern from encroaching upon its exclusive domain in Brainerd, then allowed the Brainerd & Northern Minnesota to run its passenger trains directly into the Northern Pacific Brainerd station. This was the first of several events which would ultimately bring the logging railroad into the Northern Pacific fold.

As of 1900, Brainerd & Northern Minnesota equipment included 12 locomotives all of the Mogul type; 298 logging cars; 193 flatcars; 1 boxcar; and 3

Brainerd Electric Street Railway car crossing the trestle which was destroyed by a windstorm. The illfated line handled mill workers and Brainerd & Northern Minnesota passengers between downtown Brainerd and the B&NM depot. — FRANK BUTTS COLLECTION

Northern Pacific log dump trestle on the Mississippi at Minneapolis, showing cars being dumped. (BELOW) During 1900 it was necessary to resort to all-rail movement of logs from the Leech Lake area to Minnesota in order to keep the mills from shutting down due to insufficient supply of logs via the river. Northern Pacific 0-6-0 switcher No. 939 poses with her crew before shoving a train of logs to the dump trestle. — BOTH MINNESOTA HISTORICAL SOCIETY

Snappy Minnesota & International No. 14 handled log trains over the road during her early years. She was built by the Richmond Locomotive Works and received during 1903. — ALCO HISTORIC PHOTOS

passenger cars. By then, it was undisputedly the most important logging railroad operating anywhere.

Although a sizeable portion of the logs handled over the Brainerd & Northern Minnesota were milled in Brainerd, the majority were floated down the Mississippi to mills in Minneapolis and beyond. During 1900, the Backus-Brooks Company of Minneapolis found itself unable to obtain enough logs by river transport to keep its mill operating on two shifts. Many of its own logs were stranded up the Mississippi some distance from the rear of the river drives. To overcome this frustrating problem, the company purchased several million board feet of timber from loggers operating near Walker — on the Brainerd & Northern Minnesota. The Brainerd & Northern Minnesota and the Northern Pacific agreed to deliver daily two trainloads of logs totaling 300,000 board feet. The elimination of shrinkage losses associated with river driving, which could amount to as much as 15 percent of the total amount banked in the woods, partially offset the higher cost of transportation via rail. In addition, interest savings on capital invested in logs from one year to the next was also a positive factor. River driving passed its peak, and rail transportation of logs became the rule in Minnesota.

The Minnesota & International Railway Company was incorporated under the laws of Minnesota on July 16, 1900, at the time acquiring the assets of the Brainerd & Northern Minnesota. Pushed by in-

fluential Northern Pacific stockholders who were also connected with the lumbering industry, the Minnesota & International reached the border community of International Falls during 1907. Twelve years later, in 1919, the Northern Pacific-controlled road owned 24 locomotives and 547 log cars.

On October 22, 1941, the Northern Pacific purchased at foreclosure sale the properties of the Minnesota & International. The following year, the Interstate Commerce Commission authorized the Northern Pacific to acquire the properties of the Big Fork & International Falls Railway, which had formed an integral portion of the Minnesota & International. What had started out over 60 years before as Minnesota's only narrow-gauge logging railroad was by then an important segment in the state's railway network.

A short distance north of Brainerd lay some 75,000 acres of timberlands owned by the St. Anthony Lumber Company. The company's initial plan called for construction of a logging railroad from Cross Lake to its timber holdings, which extended north approximately 30 miles to the shores of Leech Lake. Logs would be dumped into Cross Lake and floated down a stream tributary to the Mississippi. The Mississippi River would provide easy transportation to mills located at St. Anthony Falls in Minneapolis.

Accordingly, Articles of Incorporation for the Northern Mississippi Railway Company were filed on February 21, 1890, and stated the following objec-

Minnesota & International Railways No. 301 with a freight train somewhere between Bemidji and International Falls. This engine was constructed in 1901 by Schenectady for the Northern Pacific as their No. 197. No. 301 was a cross-compound Ten Wheeler with a large low pressure cylinder. — KOOCHICHING COUNTY HISTORICAL SOCIETY

An M&I way freight switches some cars in the early 1900's. This American type 4-4-0 came from parent Northern Pacific. — KOOCHICHING COUNTY HISTORICAL SOCIETY

Passengers stand around the Big Falls station platform waiting for the Minnesota & International's mixed train to depart. The four-wheeled Bobber-type caboose No. 3 appears to be of Northern Pacific ancestry. — KOOCHICHING COUNTY HISTORICAL SOCIETY

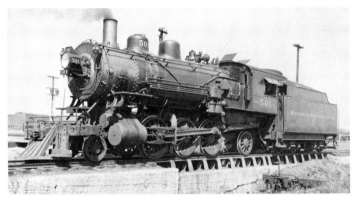

Minnesota & International No. 501, a Class T Prairie type locomotive, stands on the cinder pit track at Bemidji in 1940. — HAROLD VAN HORN COLLECTION (BELOW) No. 21 wheels a five car passenger train along the former Brainerd & Northern Minnesota line near Nisswa during the early 1900's. The first baggage car contains a Railway Post Office unit in the head end. — WAYNE C. OLSEN COLLECTION

A portion of the Brainerd Lumber Company sawmill at Brainerd. The little railway in the foreground was used to move finished lumber to the drying yard. — FRANK KING COLLECTION

tive:

> ... to build, improve and operate a railway from a point on the line between Section 8 and 9, Township 137, Range 27 in Crow Wing County, distance 550 feet, south of the quarter post on said dividing line; thence, in a northerly line to some convenient point in Section 27, Township 141, Range 28 in Cass County.

The absence of a reference to any established communities emphasized the isolated location of the operation.

The first Northern Mississippi Railway locomotive was shipped from Aitkin to Pine River aboard the steamer *Faun* and then hauled some 35 miles through the woods on logging wagons by 16 pairs of horses — a journey of three days. This balloon-stacked Porter-built Mogul carried the name *E.M. Fowler* on her cab. Fowler was an official of the Cross Lake Logging Company, a firm which logged for its owner, the St. Anthony Lumber Company, and

St. Anthony Lumber Company's first locomotive, named the *E. M. Fowler*, spots a gravel train during the construction of their logging railroad in 1890. The railroad operation became known as the Northern Mississippi Railway. The little Mogul was built by Porter in 1890. — MINNESOTA HISTORICAL SOCIETY

Cross Lake log landing on the Northern Mississippi Railway during 1904. The track at the landing was slightly canted to facilitate rolling the logs off the cars. — MINNESOTA HISTORICAL SOCIETY (BELOW) Northern Mississippi Railway engine No. 1 pulls into Cross Lake with the last train of logs, sometime during 1908. — KADIKOMEG MUSEUM

others owning timber in the area. The Northern Mississippi received a second Mogul locomotive from Porter in 1890, and a third from the same builder the following year. Logging cars numbered 100, and Northern Mississippi logging trains usually consisted of 24 cars, each train carrying some 70,000 board feet of pine. In all, the Northern Mississippi Railway constructed 28 miles of main line track laid with 45-pound rail. The road was never physically connected to any other railroad, though at one time there was talk of a connection with the Mann Lake Branch of the Brainerd & Northern Minnesota.

During 1893, the St. Anthony properties, including the Northern Mississippi Railway, were acquired by Weyerhaeuser and his associates W.H. Laird and the Nortons of Winona, Minnesota for the sum of $1,710,000, and operated as the Northland Pine Company. At the time, this represented an immense transaction. Weyerhaeuser's "cruiser," the man who estimates how much lumber a standing timber tract will cut, took 114 days to estimate the pine, which produced 500 million board feet of lumber.

Logging operations at Northland Pine Company ceased in 1908, but the Northern Mississippi, including its three locomotives and 100 logging cars, were left intact. A group of promoters and area residents did try to revive the line. Their plan was to rename it and extend it southward, either to Brainerd or to Aitkin, whichever could provide the more suitable terminal facilities. They also anticipated an extension north beyond Leech Lake, perhaps to a connection with the Great Northern near Cass Lake. This proposal to reactivate the railroad failed for want of financial support, and in 1911 the Northland Pine Company sold its 28 miles of railroad to a Minneapolis salvage firm. The locomo-

tives and cars reputedly found their way to new owners in Saskatchewan, Montana, and Chicago.

The O'Neal Brothers, logging contractors of Stillwater, Minnesota who logged for the Laird-Norton Company of Winona, constructed in 1895 a railroad somewhat similar to the Northern Mississippi. The O'Neal Brothers' road extended from their log landing on Knife River some seven miles upstream from the village of Mora, about 27 miles north to Camp A. In the years from 1889 to 1898, logging contracts with Laird-Norton totaled close to $500,000. A peak cut of 25 million board feet was attained in 1897. Logs were floated down the Knife into the Snake (which emptied into the St. Croix) and finally, by way of the Mississippi, to Laird-Norton's mill at Winona. Except for ex-Omaha Road 4-4-0 No. 262 (built by Taunton in 1880 for the St. Paul & Sioux City Railroad), what equipment was used on this road remains a mystery. Certain it is, however, that it all would have had to be hauled in overland, as the railroad did not connect physically with any other

A couple sweethearts of the engine crew pose in the cab of St. Croix Timber company Mogul No. 2. At this time the engine was operating in Douglas County, Wisconsin, circa 1912, near Bear Lake. This locomotive was constructed by Porter in 1884 for the Chippewa River & Menomonie and used next on the Empire Lumber Company's operation in Minnesota, then to Douglas County, Wisconsin — HOWARD PEDDLE COLLECTION

carrier. In 1902, by which time the Laird-Norton holdings were completely cut over, Frederick Weyerhaeuser purchased the rails for his Nebagamon Lumber Company in Wisconsin.

A few miles to the southeast of the O'Neal Brothers' logging railroad, the Empire Lumber Company of Winona operated a similar line between its timber stands on Crooked and Sand creeks and the landing at Yellow Banks on the St. Croix River. Logs were floated down the St. Croix and the Mississippi to the mill at Winona. A letter to one of Empire's officials outlining the proposal of Mr. Flemming, the company's woods superintendent, that such a line be built is reproduced herewith to show the many considerations involved:

Mr. Flemming wants to build a logging railroad to get out the timber on Crooked and Sand creeks. He says it is very doubtful about his being able to get the logs out of the creeks in the time the contract calls for. Mr. Flemming has had an engineer go over the land with him and they have followed out a line starting from the St. Croix at a good landing and find that a railroad can be built at about the average cost of logging railroads. The length of the line would be about twenty miles. We have looked over the logging roads of Goodyear & Co. at Tomah, the J.R. Davis Lbr. Co. at Phillips, the Jump River Lbr. Co. at Prentice, and find that the cost of these roads including equipments is from four to five thousand dollars per mile. The companies using logging railroads favor that way of moving logs. They say it is much more satisfactory than driving out of small creeks, and that you are certain to get the logs the season they are cut. The road will cost at the outside, one hundred thousand dollars. When the logs are all cut there will be the rails left which will be about all that will be of any value. These at the market price of old rails would come to thirty thousand dollars, or we could use them and the

A rare photograph of the log landing on O'Neil Brothers logging railroad at Knife River Dam near Mora, Minnesota. After dumping the last car of the train, the entire landing and train crew took time out to have their portraits taken for posterity. The date is just before the turn of the century. Two road locomotives, both 4-4-0's, handled three trains daily with an average of 26 cars per train. The board feet of logs per car averaged 3,300. — KANABEC COUNTY HISTORICAL SOCIETY

A string of Russel cars, loaded high with white pine logs, wait at Cuba Siding on the Great Northern Railway who will eventually pick them up for delivery to the Mississippi River. The logs were cut for the Standard Lumber Company of Dubuque, Iowa, who let a contract to the Swan River Logging Company to lot their 100,000,000 feet of pine on the Chippewa Indian Reservation between 1904 and 1908. A 17-mile logging railroad, known as the Leech Lake & Northern, was constructed off the GN at Cuba into reservation land during 1904 to handle this timber. — U.S. FOREST SERVICE

rolling stock to move out the logs on the Douglas County tract. Mr. Flemming estimates that it will cost him to put in what dams he has to have to drive the logs out of the creeks to the St. Croix ninety thousand dollars. He makes up the estimate from the cost of the dams he has already built and the cost of the logs that have been driven up to this time. We have decided that there is not enough time to try and put in the road for next winter's use. The distance from the nearest railroad station to the landing on the St. Croix is twelve miles and it is a very bad road, the rails and the engine would have to be hauled in the winter. These we would have to pay for by April or May, 1893. This, with the cost of building eight miles that would have to be put in during the summer of '93 would come to about forty thousand dollars. Mr. Flemming says that the eight miles would do for two season's work and after that three or four miles a season would have to be put in until the timber farthest from the stream was reached. He says there is timber enough near the creeks for this winter's logging that can be put in cheap as the haul is short. He wants us to decide by September 1st about building the road so that he can make arrangements for next winter's logging. The average distance these logs would

have to be moved on the road would be 14 miles. We find that the cost of moving logs this distance on logging roads is from 25 to 40 cents per 1,000 board feet so that after the road was built, the logs could be moved to the St. Croix much cheaper than by driving down the streams. We have figured on this a good deal and think that in view of the short time we have to move this timber, that it would be adviseable (sic) to build the road, but will not come to any decision until we hear what you think about it.

Construction of this railroad is believed to have begun in 1894, and eight miles of line were built that year. A new Porter Mogul plus a small saddle-tank locomotive and several logging cars, acquired from Weyerhaeuser's Mississippi River Logging Company near Chippewa Falls, were on hand when operations began. This equipment was shipped to Grantsburg, Wisconsin over the St. Paul & Duluth Railroad and sleigh hauled from there to the landing at Yellow Banks. Known locally as the "Flemming Road," it functioned until 1899, at which time rails, its three locomotives and rolling stock were shipped north to the Empire Lumber Company's new logging operation in Douglas County, south of Superior, Wisconsin.

Duluth & Northern Minnesota No. 2 rumbles across a timber trestle near Knife River on a cold winter day in 1899. This Mogul type locomotive was built by Baldwin in 1883 and sold to the Duluth & Iron Range as their No. 3. She was used by the road in laying steel between Two Harbors and the iron country. The famed little engine, now known as the *Three Spot*, is on permanent exhibition at Two Harbors, Minnesota. — ST. LOUIS COUNTY HISTORICAL SOCIETY

4

NORTH OF LAKE SUPERIOR

Large-scale logging operations along the watershed north of Lake Superior did not commence until shortly before the turn of the century. The rugged terrain and limited log-driving potential forestalled early attempts at heavy logging. Nevertheless, even before the Civil War two small local sawmill operators were already cutting timber on the north shore of the lake — timber that was not, however, considered as desirable as that to be found to the south and west of Duluth. The late 1880's and early 1890's saw a considerable amount of logging activity with winter sleigh haul transportation of logs cut along the north shore; but such operations were for the most part limited to areas within a few miles of the lake. Cut logs would be banked along the shore for the winter months and then rafted to Duluth-Superior sawmills the following summer. Log rafts later became a common sight — the largest containing as many as 6 million board feet, or the equivalent of 1,200 single-tier railroad carloads.

By 1890, most of Michigan's big white pine stands were gone and Bay City and Saginaw lumbermen were seeking new sawmill sites. Duluth, with its proximity to large stands of pine and access to lake shipping of lumber, was a natural choice, and that same year the Michigan firm of Mitchell & McClure erected a huge mill there. Reputedly the largest sawmill in the world at the time of its construction, the mill cut 54 million board feet of timber in the year 1899 alone.

Another Michigan lumbering firm, Merrill & Ring Lumber Company, commenced cutting lumber at Duluth during 1891. Its giant mill was by 1899 running Mitchell & McClure's a close second, with a cut of 51 million board feet. Merrill & Ring's owners were the major stockholders of the Cranberry Lumber Company, which logged along the Cranberry River in Wisconsin, on the south shore of Lake Superior, and during the 1890's most of the mill's logs came from that source.

The third Michigan firm to build a large mill in the Duluth region was Alger-Smith, which started producing lumber at the head of the lakes during 1898. All three of these companies owned vast timber holdings north of Lake Superior and were destined to move the bulk of their logs by rail. Of the three, Alger-Smith became by far the largest operator on Lake Superior's north shore. Its common carrier railroad, the Duluth & Northern Minnesota, was chartered on May 31, 1898, under the laws of Minnesota. In the course of its 20-year life span, it would become the most important logging railroad in the state, constructing over 99 miles of main line and approximately 350 miles of branches and spurs.

A busy 1915 scene on the Duluth & Northern Minnesota Railway at their Knife River yard. Dozens of carloads of logs are waiting to be picked up by the Duluth & Iron Range for movement to the sawmills at Duluth. Engine No. 101, at the right of the turntable, was the only Shay owned by the road. — FRANK KING COLLECTION

An 1890's view showing the Merrill & Ring (Saginaw Lumber Company) and Mitchell & McClure sawmills in West Duluth. Little remains today along the waterfront to remind one of what was once Duluth's most important industry — lumbering. — ST. LOUIS COUNTY HISTORICAL SOCIETY (LEFT) General Russell A. Alger, shown at his desk in Washington, was Secretary of War in addition to heading up the lumber firm of Alger, Smith & Company. — LIBRARY OF CONGRESS

The *Duluth News Tribune* for May 13, 1898 gave the following account of the coming of the road:

ALGER ROAD TO BE BUILT . . . Duluth is to have a new railroad known as the Duluth and Northern Minnesota. Surveyors are now in the field and within 30 or 40 days the work of grading the line will be in progress . . . The promoters of the road are no less a firm than Alger, Smith & Co., the well-known Michigan lumbermen. Mr. M.S. Smith of the company is president of the railroad company and is a prominent banker in Detroit. General Alger of the lumber company is the present Secretary of War. The work of getting the railroad under way has been conducted largely by John Millen, a Detroit capitalist and a man that has long been connected with Alger, Smith & Co.

Russell A. Alger was Governor of Michigan from 1885 to 1887, and later gained national prominence as Secretary of War in the cabinet of President William McKinley at the time of the Spanish-American War. In 1903, he was elected to the United States Senate. Alger had started a lumber business in Grand Rapids, Michigan in 1860, just in time to have his enterprise ruined by financial problems incident to the beginning of the Civil War. Enlisting in the army as a private, he emerged four years later a major general.

The first year of the Duluth & Northern Minnesota operation saw the completion of 7.5 miles of road into the woods from Knife River, a community on Lake Superior about 20 miles north of Duluth. At Knife River, a connection was made with the Duluth & Iron Range Railroad over which Alger-Smith's logs were transported to the mill at Duluth. Motive power and rolling stock on the Duluth & Northern Minnesota initially consisted of two Mogul-type locomotives and 100 logging cars. These cars, originally equipped with small-diameter wheels, were rebuilt about 1908 (in order to meet inter-change requirements) using trucks with larger wheels procured from scrapped Duluth & Iron Range wooden ore cars. Unfortunately, after their rebuilding, they

Duluth & Northern Minnesota's first locomotive pauses at Kane Siding in order for the train crew to set retainers on the log cars before descending the two percent grade into Knife River. The engine came from Alger-Smith's Manistique Railway in Michigan. — ST. LOUIS COUNTY HISTORICAL SOCIETY (BELOW) A McGiffert log loader is hard at work on a D&NM, spur in Lake County. Note the empty cars to the rear of the machine which are pulled through as required for loading. — FRANK KING COLLECTION

Alger-Smith's tug *Ada* towing a log boom along the north shore of Lake Superior. These logs were cut near Pigeon River beyond the reach of the D&NM. — FRANK KING COLLECTION (LEFT) Loggers often displayed great ingenuity in coping with adverse situations. This chute enabled logs to bypass the High Falls of the Pigeon River on their way to Lake Superior. — MINNESOTA HISTORICAL SOCIETY

Duluth & Northern Minnesota No. 12 rests on a Sunday afternoon in the woods. The engine watchman and his lady friends stand by the stack for the camera. — DENNIS OJARD

Alger-Smith's Manistique Railway engine No. 3 in Michigan. The locomotive was constructed by the Baldwin Locomotive Works in 1890. — C. T. STONER COLLECTION

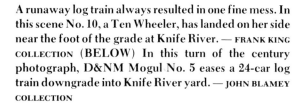

A runaway log train always resulted in one fine mess. In this scene No. 10, a Ten Wheeler, has landed on her side near the foot of the grade at Knife River. — FRANK KING COLLECTION (BELOW) In this turn of the century photograph, D&NM Mogul No. 5 eases a 24-car log train downgrade into Knife River yard. — JOHN BLAMEY COLLECTION

A southbound mixed on the Duluth & Northern Minnesota, listed on the time table as train No. 2, swings around a curve, then slows to pick-up passengers at Lax Lake.

Lumberjacks and others await the Duluth & Northern Minnesota train at Alger which will take them into the woods. These travelers had arrived via the Duluth & Iron Range, whose main line overhead bridge may be seen in the background. (LEFT) Passengers scurry aboard a D&NM train at Lax Lake. (BELOW) The skater in this photograph is more intent on the photographer than observing the D&NM mixed train passing by Lax Lake in the background — GEORGE WAXLAW COLLECTION

An old-time circuit camera records on film a record Duluth & Iron Range Rail Road train of logs near the Virginia & Rainy Lake sawmill at West Duluth, on April 8, 1910. The train, handled by 4-8-0 No. 62 between the Duluth & Northern Minnesota interchange at Knife River and Duluth, consisted of 66 Russel log cars carrying a total of 330,000 feet of logs in board measure. This was the largest train of logs hauled into Duluth and likely the largest of its type ever handled in Minnesota. — LAKE COUNTY HISTORICAL SOCIETY

were prone to jump the track when operated over jerry-built temporary logging spurs laid with light rail.

By 1899, Duluth & Northern Minnesota trackage had increased to 15 miles. In addition, the company blanketed the forest lying immediately north and west of Knife River with an extensive system of branches and temporary spurs. That same year saw the introduction of a steam log loader, capable of loading about 30 cars per day with one gang of men. Under the old system, three gangs and three teams had been required to load the same number of cars. At the time, Alger-Smith was also logging along the Pigeon River near the Canadian border, and logs were towed from the mouth of Pigeon River to Duluth in rafts of 5 million board feet enclosed in a bag-type boom.

To the Alger-Smith enterprise, the logging railroad was no novelty. Back in 1886, on the opposite shore of Lake Superior, it had chartered and built the Manistique Railway to move its logs in northern Michigan. Nicknamed "The Myrtle Navy" (after a popular smoking tobacco of the time), the Manistique Railway during 1905 reached a maximum size of 51 miles of main line with 27 miles of branches. In 1910 it discontinued operation of its line between Seney, Michigan — on the Duluth, South Shore & Atlantic Railway — and the Alger-Smith mill at Grand Marais on Lake Superior. The Manistique was offered for sale, but when no buyers appeared, its owners shipped much of the rail and equipment to Knife River for use in facilitating expanding Duluth & Northern Minnesota operations.

Construction of the Duluth & Northern Minnesota proceeded at a rapid pace, and by 1901 there were 46 miles of main line in operation. During 1902, Alger-Smith was conducting heavy logging operations north of Two Harbors in the vicinity of Highland. Spurs were constructed off the Duluth & Iron

Range's Drummond branch into this timber, built mainly to log long pilings destined for Chicago, Milwaukee & St. Paul ore dock construction at Escanaba, Michigan. That year, the Duluth & Northern Minnesota acquired from Mitchell & McClure 13 miles of logging railroad extending north from the Duluth & Iron Range near York, intending to incorporate this trackage into its main line. However, this plan was subsequently rejected, and the main line was constructed to the south through Clarke. Two years later, the end of the track was at mile post 73. The building of the Duluth & Northern Minnesota was of major importance to the timber industry in Duluth, for in addition to handling timber for the parent company, it hauled logs for many other lumber concerns operating along its lines. One of these, the Virginia & Rainy Lake Company, used its own locomotives in logging operations off the Duluth & Northern Minnesota near the Gooseberry River.

In the first two miles out of Knife River, the Duluth & Northern Minnesota climbed 200 feet, making it necessary for all northbound trains to double the grade between there and Kane Siding. Before proceeding down the two percent grade into Knife River, southbound log trains stopped at Kane Siding to set up retainers. (A retainer is a small valve usually located near the brake wheel at the end of the car, by means of which a certain portion of the brake cylinder pressure may be retained to aid in retarding the acceleration of a train descending long grades, while the brake pipe pressure is increased after one application to recharge the auxiliary reservoirs on the cars in the train.) Up the line, southbound log trains were forced to double the 4.5-mile grade between Clarke and Alger, where the line passed under the Duluth & Iron Range.

The Duluth & Northern Minnesota crossed many superb trout streams, all of which emptied into Lake Superior. The country was a trout fisherman's

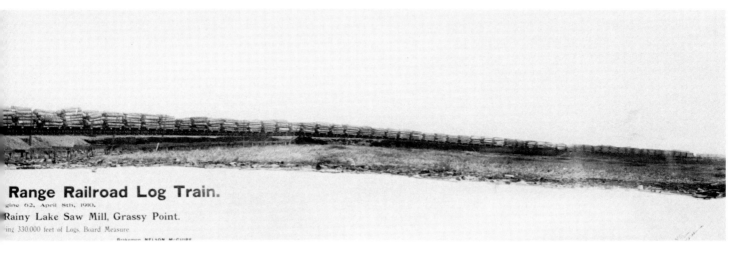

Range Railroad Log Train.

gine 62, April 8th, 1910.
Rainy Lake Saw Mill, Grassy Point.
ing 330,000 feet of Logs, Board Measure
Brakemen NELSON McGUIRE

Looking across the river from the D&NM yard towards the community of Knife River in 1915. By then pulpwood was an important commodity moving over the road. — FRANK KING COLLECTION

For each cash fare paid, the Duluth & Northern Minnesota conductors were required to issue a passenger cash fare receipt indicating direction traveled, between what stations and amount of fare paid. — FRANK KING COLLECTION

paradise, and the railroad occasionally ran special excursion trains especially for fishermen. In this connection, an eye-catching advertisement appeared in the *Duluth News Tribune* for May 4, 1908:

Fishing Excursion, Sunday, May 14, via Duluth & Northern Minnesota Railway . . . Special train connection with Duluth & Iron Range leaving Duluth 7:45 A.M. returning 4:45 P.M. Stopping at Knife River, Stewart River, Encampment River, Gooseberry River, Split Rock River . . .

By 1909, the Duluth & Northern Minnesota was offering passenger service, in the form of a mixed train to Finland, Minnesota. Here, connections with a stage line could be made for many lakeside points. At the time, there was no road along the north shore of Lake Superior, and — with the exception of fishing vessels and the mail boat which plied between Duluth and various north shore points — the Duluth & Northern Minnesota provided the only direct connection with the outside world. During that year, the company purchased the Akeley and Sprague timber tract in Cook County, comprising over 1 billion board feet of the best remaining white pine in the state. Through this purchase, Alger-Smith assured itself of continued activity for at least another decade. Logging was now at its peak, with the logging railroad handling six to eight trains of logs daily to Knife River, where a concrete dock was constructed for receiving inbound coal shipments and for transferring pulpwood from railroad cars to lake vessels for shipment to eastern paper mills. The wave-battered remains of this old dock jut out into Lake Superior to this day.

By 1910 rails had been pushed to the Manitou River country. The main logging operations reached Lax Lake, Maple, and Finland, and from 1912 to 1915 they centered around Cramer. As logging advanced further north, the older spurs were picked up and the steel rails relaid at the site of new operations. During 1912, the company picked up the steel on the important Mile 48 branch. Most of the spurs south of this point had been removed previously.

Baldwin built Ten Wheeler No. 11 spots cars of pulpwood on the Duluth & Northern Minnesota dock at Knife River for reloading onto the steamer *Lackawanna* during 1915. The storm battered remains of the old dock can still be seen today. — FRANK KING COLLECTION (RIGHT) Engine No. 2 switches former D&IR wooden ore cars for coal loading at the Knife River dock.— U.S. CORPS OF ENGINEERS - DULUTH

Duluth & Northern Minnesota No. 14 drifts downgrade into Knife River with 35 carloads of white pine logs. This locomotive had just arrived from the Baldwin Locomotive Works when this scene was taken in 1913 and the engine would carry the same number under three owners during the next 60 years of service. Old No. 14 has been preserved for posterity and is being restored presently for display at the Lake Superior Museum of Transportation at Duluth. — FRANK KING COLLECTION

It was the fond hope of Duluth & Northern Minnesota president and general manager John Millen to extend the line to connect with the Port Arthur, Duluth & Western Railway near the Canadian border, thereby creating a direct route between Duluth and the Canadian lakehead cities of Fort William and Port Arthur. Around 1912, plans for this extension reached such serious proportions that the company considered ordering six Mikado-type locomotives from the Baldwin Locomotive Works to handle the anticipated traffic over the proposed connection, although it subsequently ordered only two. At about the same time, however, two events took place which dimmed all prospects for such an extension. First, completion of the Canadian Northern-controlled Duluth, Winnipeg & Pacific between Fort Frances and Duluth (in 1912) provided a direct rail connection between Duluth and Canada. Second, the owners of Alger-Smith elected to invest in Alabama and Florida timberlands and the up-and-coming automobile industry in Detroit. Indeed, the Alger-Sullivan Lumber Company then organized by Alger was for many years one of the most important lumber companies operating in the state of Florida.

Business car *Grand Marais* of the D&NM was photographed on the Florida East Coast Railway's Key West Extension during 1912. Posing on the platform is President and General Manager John Millen (third from the left). The car was originally used on Alger-Smith's Manistique Railway in Michigan. — JOHN A. STEPHENSON, JR. COLLECTION

A mixed train on Canadian Northern's Gunflint Branch, pulled by Mogul No. 108 takes the siding at Whitefish, Ontario, in 1918. This line was constructed as the Port Arthur, Duluth & Western and played a prominent role in at least three schemes for a direct rail link between Duluth and the Canadian lakehead cities of Fort William and Port Arthur which was never completed. — THUNDER BAY HISTORICAL MUSEUM SOCIETY

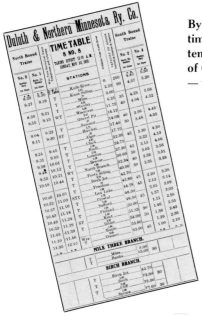

By 1910, the date of this D&NM time table, the railroad extended to Cramer, a distance of 62 miles from Knife River. — WAYNE C. OLSEN COLLECTION

At Alger the Duluth & Northern Minnesota rails passed under the double track main line of the Duluth & Iron Range. —DM&IR HISTORICAL COLLECTION

Three-truck Lima Shay No. 101 was the only geared engine on the Duluth & Northern Minnesota. Capable of ascending 10 to 12 percent grades, she came in handy on some of the roller coaster logging spurs north of Lake Superior. — FRANK KING COLLECTION

Sleigh loading at Alger-Smith Camp No. 8 in Cook County. The logs were moved perhaps two or three miles for reloading onto D&NM cars for the 100 mile plus railroad haul to the mills at Duluth. — FRANK KING COLLECTION

An early 1900 era view looking towards Garfield Avenue showing grain elevators and rail yards in Duluth. The Alger-Smith sawmill and lumber piles can be seen at the foot of the Interstate Bridge in the distance. — FRANK KING COLLECTION

Peak Duluth & Northern Minnesota equipment ownership was attained in 1911, at which time there were ten rod engines and one Lima Shay on the roster. The ten rod engines averaged 54 tons each and developed an average tractive effort of 22,048 pounds. Rolling stock consisted of 374 logging cars, 47 flatcars, 8 coal cars, 4 boxcars, 2 passenger cars, and 16 company service cars, including 9 cabooses. To assist in moving peak log traffic during the winter months, the road often supplemented its motive power fleet by leasing Class G Consolidations from the Duluth & Iron Range. The Duluth & Northern Minnesota main line was laid with 60-pound rail, and the branches and spurs with 45- and 56- pound steel.

In 1916, the big logging operations were in Cook County at Cascade. During 1918, the road moved 423,340 tons of freight and carried 14,863 passengers, and that same year it reached mile post 99.25. As logging operations moved north, however, transportation costs — and with them management's concern as to the viability of its enterprise — continued to climb. To reduce expenses, John Millen came up with a plan to extend the Duluth & Northern Minnesota from mile post 99 to Grand Marais on Lake Superior, where construction of a new sawmill was contemplated. This would have shortened the rail haul by almost 100 miles, and permitted abandonment or sale of a substantial portion of the road between Cascade and Knife River. Finished lumber

D&NM's No. 2, with a boiler full of steam, prepares to leave Knife river for a days work in the woods. The date is circa 1913. — FRANK KING COLLECTION

Rail removal crew poses with Duluth & Northeastern Mogul No. 21 during D&NM salvage operations in 1923. — E. A. KRUGER COLLECTION

would then have been shipped out of Grand Marais by lake vessel. Mile post 99.25, though, was destined to become the end of the line for the Duluth & Northern Minnesota. By 1919, the big Alger-Smith cutting show in the Minnesota woods was all over.

Most logging railroads were tagged with nicknames — if not complimentary, at least colorful — and the "Gut and Liver Route" appellation for the Minneapolis & Rainy River mentioned earlier was only one of many such. The up-and-down-hill Duluth & Northeastern was aptly tagged the "Damn Narrow Escape," and the Duluth & Northern Minnesota was known to lumberjacks as the "Gunnysack line." In the latter instance the reference was culinary, for no fresh beef was available in the camps in the early years, and the meat served in those of Alger-Smith consisted largely of salt pork, sowbelly, and corned beef, all of which came wrapped in a burlap-like material.

On July 15, 1921, the Duluth & Northern Minnesota received permission from the Interstate Commission to abandon its line. The following year, *Railway Age* for September 16 reported:

DULUTH & NORTHERN MINNESOTA SOLD . . . This railroad extending from Knife River, Minn., to Mile post, 99.25 miles, has been sold to R. Waldron. On July 15, 1921, the Interstate Commerce Commission authorized the abandonment of the entire railroad. It is planned to use the D&NM as a nucleus for the construction of the Duluth & Ontario, which will extend from Duluth, Minn., to Fort William, Ont. (Canada), a distance of 216 miles. Mr. Waldron will be president of the new company and will be associated with a number of Duluth and Minneapolis men, among them being H. Baxter, of Minneapolis, attorney of the Duluth, Winnipeg & Pacific; M.J. Dooley, of Minneapolis, general manager of the Minneapolis, Northfield & Southern, and R.M. Hunter of Duluth and James S. Sebree of Pierre, S.D.

The Duluth & Ontario project, however, never materialized. A short time afterwards, the northern por-

Finis for the Duluth & Northern Minnesota. The last steel was loaded on D&NE cars on November 30, 1923. — E. A. KRUGER COLLECTION

74

Merrill & Ring's big tug *Gladiator* handled log booms from their Split Rock Lumber Company at the mouth of Split Rock River to the mill at Duluth. — HARVEY MILLER COLLECTION (BELOW) A typical small, two-truck Climax geared locomotive used in the woods. — BENJAMIN F. G. KLINE, JR.

A builder's view of Split Rock Lumber Company Climax locomotive No. 3. Power was supplied by a pair of cylinders to rods connecting a flywheel and then, through an arrangement of longitudinal rods and universal joints, transmitted to gear sets on the axles of each truck. — JOHN E. LEWIS COLLECTION FROM BENJAMIN F. G. KLINE, JR.

tion of the Duluth & Northern Minnesota road, including the rails on the remainder, was sold to the General Logging Company of Cloquet, Minnesota, which used this trackage to extend its line into the last remaining big timber north of Lake Superior. On May 14, 1923, Duluth & Northeastern engine No. 21, a veteran Mogul used in Panama Canal construction, left Cloquet with a train consisting of one coach and five flatcars and made its way to the end of the line at Cascade. This train and its crew began the job of taking up the steel on the branches between Cascade and mile post 69.5, at which point the main line was severed. The line between mile post 69.5 and Cascade was left intact and became part of General Logging's main line. By November 30, 1923 main line steel between mile post 69.5 and Knife River had been removed, to be later used by General Logging in constructing the portion of its line extending from the end of the Duluth & Northeastern at Hornby to mile post 69.5 on the Duluth & Northern Minnesota. In addition to engine No. 21, Duluth & Northeastern engines No. 2 and No. 20 were also used on the dismantling job. With the removal of the Duluth & Northern Minnesota, there passed from the scene the most notable of Minnesota's colorful common carrier logging railroads.

During 1899, Merrill & Ring formed the Split Rock Lumber Company to log 200 million board feet of timber recently acquired from the Gratwick, Smith, and Fryer interests. That same year saw the start of construction of its logging railroad, extending from the mouth of the Split Rock River some ten miles north into the woods.

The first 1.9 miles from Lake Superior were incorporated as the Split Rock & Northern Railroad, so as to exempt the log dump trestle, terminal and shop buildings from property taxation, that portion of the road being considered a common carrier and thus falling under the state's railroad gross earnings tax

instead. This however, did not deter zealous local authorities from imposing taxes on the property to the tune of $1,500 for the three years ending in 1906.

Log trains were dumped on a trestle at the mouth of the river into a cribbed-off area, from which the logs were sluiced into the lake and made up into rafts for towing to the mill at Duluth by an ocean-type tug named *Gladiator*. An interesting feature of the tug operation was the use of carrier pigeons to fly distress messages to the company offices. Split Rock motive power consisted of a Mogul (ex-Cranberry

Split Rock Lumber Company headquarters close to the Split Rock River, showing the enginehouse, storehouse and camps in 1907. — JOHN FRITZEN COLLECTION

The famed Worlds Fair Load, containing 36,055 board feet of timber in 50 logs, was cut in Michigan by the Estate of Thomas Nestor for the 1893 Columbian Exposition in Chicago. Seven years later, this firm constructed a logging railroad to reach timber north of Lake Superior in Minnesota. — MINNESOTA HISTORICAL SOCIETY

Lumber Company Ltd. No. 4) and two Climax-geared locomotives. With but one known exception, these were only Climax locomotives to operate in Minnesota. The *Mississippi Valley Lumberman* for December 14, 1900 gives the following account concerning acquisition of the first of them:

The Split Rock Lumber Company, which is logging at the river of that name on the north shore of the lake, has just received from the makers a Climax geared locomotive of 25 tons, the first of its kind in use hereabouts. All the wheels are drivers connected by gearing. It is said to work well. There is a 4-½ percent grade on the company's road out of the landing for several miles, and a geared engine seemed necessary for climbing it.

Logging operations on the Split Rock ceased during 1906, and the railroad was removed the following year. In its final annual report, the Split Rock Lumber Company listed the following railroad assets, totaling $4,874:

One 35-ton Climax engine	$2,000.00
One 28-ton Climax engine	1,500.00
8 old logging cars @ $100 each	800.00
2 hand cars @ $10 each	20.00
3 flat cars, 1 snow plow and 1 push car	50.00
42,000 feet trestle timbers	504.00

(The above is included primarily to show values placed on second hand logging railroad equipment at the time. Because of the 4-½ percent grade, all locomotives and cars were equipped with air brakes, although link and pin couplers were used throughout the life of the operation.)

Split Rock Lumber Company's operation was considered highly successful by its owners, with net profits totaling $863,454 over its seven-year life. By contrast, parent company Merrill & Ring's Cranberry Lumber Company, which operated in Wisconsin on the opposite shore of Lake Superior from 1891 to 1900, was a loser.

Merrill & Ring also staged a logging operation off the Duluth, Missabe & Northern Railway near Saginaw, about 20 miles north of Duluth. Logs were handled by the Duluth, Missabe & Northern to the mill at West Duluth. Upon completion of logging along the Split Rock, however, the company moved to British Columbia.

Nearby, along the Gooseberry River, the Estate of Thomas Nestor, a large Michigan lumbering firm, in 1900 acquired the entire north shore timber holdings of Knight and Vilas, totaling 250 million board feet of pine, at a price of $4.00 per thousand board feet. Included in the $1,250,000 transaction was the

Knight and Vilas mill in Ashland, Wisconsin. Financial backing was provided by the big Calumet & Hecla Copper Company of Calumet, Michigan, for whom most of the lumber was destined.

By January 1901 the Nestors were employing 400 men in their north shore camps. Eleven miles of railroad had already been constructed for delivering logs to the mouth of the Gooseberry River on Lake Superior. One branch of the railroad extended north along the Gooseberry watershed to Section 31-55-10, and another extended to Section 8-55-9, where it later connected with and crossed the Duluth & Northern Minnesota Railway. (Alger-Smith's Duluth & Northern Minnesota later used a portion of the latter grade in constructing its Greenwood Lake Branch.) Little is known of the Nestor railroad equipment other than the fact that the company operated three locomotives and 57 logging cars. One engine was a diamond-stacked Mogul which, according to local legend, had been exhibited at the Chicago World's Fair of 1893.

Near the mouth of the Gooseberry River, a balloon loop track served to turn trains. Log cars were dumped from a ledge blasted out of the rock along the west bank of the river, their contents cascading some 70 feet into the water below. From the river's mouth, logs were towed in extremely large booms across Lake Superior to Nestor mills in Ashland, Wisconsin and Baraga, Michigan. The tow to Baraga, the longest undertaking on Lake Superior at the time, was all without shelter, around treacherous Keweenaw Point, a distance of 230 miles. During 1901, the Nestor Company handled a log raft contain-

The photographer was subject to frostbite when he exposed Shay No. 4 of the Mitchell & McClure Logging Railroad paused in the woods with a train of white pine logs. The location is Carlton County about 20 miles southwest of Duluth. Note the extra water car behind the engine in this mid-1890's scene. — FRANK KING COLLECTION

ing 6 million board feet between Two Harbors and Baraga, the largest ever floated on Lake Superior.

The winter of 1901-1902 witnessed 800 men at work in five camps on the north shore. By spring 50 million board feet of logs were banked at the mouth of the Gooseberry, awaiting towing across the lake. By then 14 miles of main line railroad were in use. Nestor logging operations on the Gooseberry ceased during 1909, and the railroad was removed.

Mitchell & McClure made extensive use of logging railroads in the area around Duluth. The company's biggest operation was in Carlton County, about 20 miles southwest of the city, and there, in 1891, an elaborate logging railroad system was constructed to reach a remarkable stand of timber along the Nemadji River that contained 500 million board feet of white pine. At Barker, connection was made with the Northern Pacific Railway, over which Mitchell & McClure obtained running rights to Pokegama Junction near Superior. Beyond the junction, Mitchell & McClure had its own line extending to the log landing trestle at Pokegama Bay on the St. Louis River. From the landing, it was only a short distance downstream to the big mill on the bayfront at West Duluth. Logging trains between Barker and Pokegama Bay were handled by an ex-Pennsylvania

Brooks-built Mogul No. 2 of Mitchell & McClure shared main line log hauling duties with an ex-Pennsylvania Railroad class H-1 Consolidation. Both engines were sold in 1901 to the Duluth & Northern Minnesota Railway. — FRANK KING COLLECTION

Mitchell & McClure lumberjacks take time out for lunch alongside a cribbed log railroad trestle. The structure is similar to the trestle shown in the end papers of this book. — UNIVERSITY OF MINNESOTA, DULUTH LIBRARY

Railroad 2-8-0 locomotive (PRR Class I "HI"). This engine was equipped with an Altoona-type firebox and created considerable interest among railroaders in the area, who appropriately dubbed it the *Pennsylvania Fantail.*

The rail line out of Barker included a number of large bridges spanning many deep ravines, some of them constructed by an unusual method of cribbing up logs. The huge structure over the Black Hoof River, which contained some 1-½ million board feet of logs, stood over 100 feet high at the river, and extended 45 rods in length. When the railroad was removed, all logs from the bridge were salvaged and taken to the mill for cutting into lumber.

In November 1901 the *Mississippi Valley Lumberman* ran an interesting account of an on-going dispute between Carlton and St. Louis counties over payment of taxes on this line. Carlton County reasoned that inasmuch as the road was located within its boundaries, the taxes should be payable to Carlton County. St. Louis County, for its part, argued that because Mitchell & McClure's headquarters were in Duluth, St. Louis County should be the recipient of its tax payments. The matter was placed before the State Auditor, who ruled in favor of Carlton County.

During 1899 Mitchell & McClure constructed a 12-mile logging railroad extending northeasterly from Adolph on the Duluth, Missabe & Northern Railway. At Adolph, log trains were turned over to the Duluth, Missabe & Northern for forwarding to the mill in West Duluth. The following year this line was abandoned, and in 1901 the grade was acquired by Brooks-Scanlon Lumber Company's Minnesota & North Wisconsin Railroad to form part of its main line.

Mitchell & McClure's last logging railroad, 13 miles in length, was built during 1901 and connected with the Duluth & Iron Range near York. One year later the company sold its interests to Alger-Smith for $750,000, the sale including the mill at Duluth, 60 million board feet of pine, and 13 miles of railroad. Along with the logging railroad, Alger-Smith acquired two locomotives, 83 logging cars, a steam log loader, and a snow plow.

A runaway log train leaves one whale of a big mess. In this scene all that is left when a Missabe Road log train overturned at the foot of Proctor Hill in Duluth in 1899. The train originated on Mitchell & McClure near Adolph. — FRANK KING COLLECTION

M. Joseph Scanlon   **Lester Brooks**   **Dwight Brooks**   **Henry Gipson**

The entrepreneurs of Brooks-Scanlon and Scanlon-Gipson were featured collectively in the 1902 issue of *Men of Minnesota*. These men also presided over the affairs of their Minnesota & North Wisconsin Railroad. — MINNESOTA HISTORICAL SOCIETY

In December 1894, as a result of the Great Hinckley Fire which devastated a vast portion of the pine forests of central Minnesota, a lumbering concern was formed in Minneapolis under the name of the Scanlon-Gipson Lumber Company, with M.J. Scanlon; H.E. Gipson; D.F., L.R., and A.S. Brooks as officers and directors. This new company acquired 80 million board feet of timber in the fire-swept area and promptly erected, at Nickerson on the Eastern Minnesota Railway, a sawmill which specialized in cutting Norway long joists and timbers. Initially, logs were railed from the Hinckley area to the mill.

In 1895 Scanlon-Gipson constructed a logging railroad to reach nearby timber stands. Three years later, on February 3, 1898, this was organized as the Minnesota & North Wisconsin Railroad. Minnesota & North Wisconsin officers included D.F. Brooks,

president; M.I. Scanlon, vice-president; L.R. Brooks, treasurer; and A.S. Brooks, superintendent. An amusing reference to the new line appeared about that time in the *Mississippi Valley Lumberman,* wherein the editor acknowledged receipt of annual passes from a number of logging railroads:

This thing of lumber companies owning and operating lines of railroad and issuing annual passes over them is getting to be quite common nowadays . . . Only the other day, the Scanlon-Gipson Lumber Company incorporated their seven miles of logging railroad as the Minnesota & North Wisconsin Railroad, and annual passes over it will be forthcoming in a few days. The passes will be alright, but as I understand it, passengers, for the present at least, will be compelled to ride in a boxcar. There are

Buildings of the early day sawmill town of Nickerson were strung out along both sides of the Eastern Minnesota Railway. The outhouse at the right corner of this illustration, was certainly a long walk during a Minnesota winter. — DOUGLAS COUNTY HISTORICAL SOCIETY

Minnesota & North Wisconsin No. 12, a handsome 4-4-0 type steam locomotive, is about to depart for the mill at Nickerson with a train of Norway pine logs. This is the only photograph of M&NW's operation at Nickerson that has surfaced to date. — MINNESOTA HISTORICAL SOCIETY

lots of other lumber roads in Minnesota and Wisconsin that issue annual passes, and the man who gets passes from all of them has his pockets as full as a Klondike gold hunter's.

The initial portion of the Scanlon-Gipson railroad ran easterly approximately six miles, from the company's mill at Nickerson towards the Wisconsin state line. In the fall of 1897 the line was extended in the opposite direction, from Nickerson to Lake Graham, a distance of five miles for a total of 11 miles of main line. Later that year a crossing was installed over the Eastern Minnesota at Nickerson, connecting both segments of the road. The inclusion of "North Wisconsin" in the corporate title of the road lends support to the belief that the parent company also owned timber holdings in nearby Wisconsin and intended to extend its railroad into that state. At this time the Minnesota & North Wisconsin owned two locomotives and 35 cars, and tracks were laid with 48- and 65- pound rail.

By 1901 Scanlon-Gipson was in control of sawmills at Nickerson, Minneapolis, and Cass Lake with an annual capacity of 150 million board feet — a far cry from its position just seven years earlier when the little mill at Nickerson produced only 17 million board feet of lumber — and also owned some 17,000 acres of Oregon pine lands purchased in 1898 as insurance against the day when Minnesota logging would become a phenomenon of the past.

The Brooks-Scanlon Lumber Company was organized in January of 1901, with M.J. Scanlon and the Brooks brothers as its principal stockholders. The

The pass, an annual exchange of courtesy to other railroads, politicians, etc., were issued by Minnesota's logging railroads. Lumbermen exercised little restraint in exchanging these colorful passes with main line carriers. — FRANK KING COLLECTION

Eastern Minnesota Railway Rogers-built Mogul No. 204 hauled logs to the Scanlon-Gipson sawmill at Nickerson and handled countless carloads of finished lumber on the way to market. No. 204 is shown in this 1890's view on the turntable at Superior, Wisconsin. — **WAYNE C. OLSEN COLLECTION**

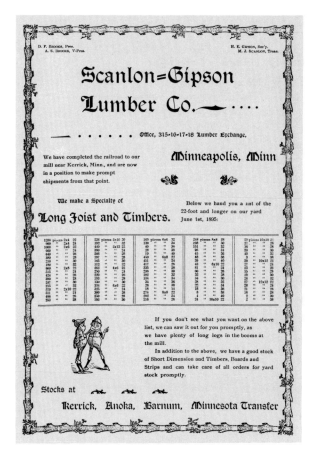

Scanlon-Gipson advertisement as it appeared in an 1895 issue of the *Mississippi Valley Lumberman*. The firm specialized in rectangular-sectioned lumber (joists) and large timber.

A portion of the Brooks-Scanlon mill looking northeast. The main mill building on the left was 250 feet in length and housed a single gang, three band plant. M&NW No. 12 pulls loaded cars of lumber from the curing yards. This 4-4-0 is the same engine as shown on the opposite page. — **DOUGLAS COUNTY HISTORICAL SOCIETY**

By 1902, Scanlon was a bustling community of some 1,200 inhabitants. In the background may be seen the Brooks-Scanlon mill and lumber storage yards. — MRS. L. RIEL COLLECTION

The town of Scanlon proper was situated on top of the hill overlooking the mill. — MRS. L. RIEL COLLECTION

objective of this new concern was to construct a mill at Scanlon, Minnesota, tributary to large quantities of recently acquired timber north of Duluth. The original intent was to erect a two-band mill, but with holdings then approaching one billion board feet, management decided instead to put up one of the largest and most modern plants in the entire country. When completed, the big mill consisted of a three-band and one gang plant, whose capacity "without crowding" was proudly stated to be 350,000 board feet for a ten-hour shift. By 1902 Scanlon had become a thriving communtiy of some 1,200 inhabitants.

To supply its new mill with logs, Brooks-Scanlon drew up plans for a common carrier railroad extending from Scanlon some 40 miles north into the timberlands. The reason for this was two-fold: First, the Cloquet and St. Louis rivers were already overcrowded much of the time with logs for the five busy Cloquet mills located only three miles upstream from Scanlon. Second, Brooks-Scanlon did not relish the possibility of having to shut down its expensive mill for lack of logs due to low water, a situation which was proving an increasing annoyance to the mill operators at Cloquet.

This graceful looking little Mikado type locomotive No. 6 carried the Brooks-Scanlon Lumber Company name at their Oregon operation. This motive power was far more modern than anything used by the Minnesota & North Wisconsin in Minnesota. — FRANK KING COLLECTION

Delaware, Lackawanna & Western No. 7 was similar to engines sold to the Minnesota & North Wisconsin. Note the unusual side water tank below the cab. — GERALD M. BEST COLLECTION (BELOW) M&NW No. 9 in service with a pony truck. — FRANK KING COLLECTION

To finance the new line out of Scanlon, the Minnesota & North Wisconsin made application to increase its captial stock from $10,000 to $350,000. While the line was not physically connected to the original Minnesota & North Wisconsin road out of Nickerson, it was built and operated under the same charter. Late 1901 saw some 500 men at work grading the roadbed, and new 56-pound rails, ordered from the Carnegie Steel Corporation, were laid on the main line that fall and winter. Taking advantage of ten miles of railroad grade built by Mitchell & McClure only two years before, the Minnesota & North Wisconsin was able to accomplish completion of 40 miles of main line by January 1, 1902. Even the ties on the former Mitchell & McClure grade remained in place, thus sparing the Minnesota & North Wisconsin another expense. (A short time after completion of the mill at Scanlon, the M&NW lines at Nickerson were abandoned — although a portion of the line was used by a local mill operator for a few years.)

By 1907 the Minnesota & North Wisconsin main line had been pushed northeasterly from Scanlon to Corolan, a distance of 44.5 miles. Branches extended from Alden Junction to the hoist on Alden Lake, 3.5 miles; from Gallagher Junction to Gallagher Lake, 1.0 miles; from Sucker River to Section 13, Township 52, and Range 13, 5.1 miles; and from Adolph Junction to the Duluth, Missabe & Northern connection at Adolph, 1.2 miles for a total of 55.3 miles of railroad.

The 3.5-mile branch between Alden Junction and Alden Lake was constructed in 1904. Brooks-Scanlon controlled large timber stands along the Cloquet River some distance north and east of its Minnesota & North Wisconsin and intended to float logs from there to Alden Lake, where they would be loaded onto cars for rail movement to Scanlon. Cloquet lumbermen under Weyerhaeuser direction, however, objected to this plan, claiming that a sorting works on the Cloquet River would interfere with

Minnesota & North Wisconsin No. 296 on the main line north of Duluth. The Omaha Road boxcar behind the locomotive contained provisions for Brooks-Scanlon logging camps. The engine was built by Cooke in 1882 for the Delaware, Lackawanna & Western as their No. 296. With the exception of a Heisler, all motive power was acquired secondhand and retained the road number of the previous owners. — RAY NOYES COLLECTION

The enginehouse and servicing facilities of the Minnesota & North Wisconsin at Scanlon about 1906. The engine at the extreme right was Duluth, Virginia & Rainy Lake Mogul No. 11, just recently purchased when this picture was taken. — FRANK KING COLLECTION

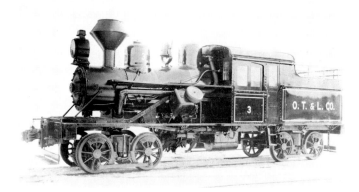

With exception of the diamond stack and headlight, Oregon Timber & Lumber Company No. 3 was almost identical to the Brooks-Scanlon's Heisler. Power was transmitted from the two v-mounted cylinders to a longitudinal driveshaft which was geared to the inner axles of each truck. — HOWARD PEDDLE COLLECTION (UPPER LEFT) M&NW's Heisler spots cars at the Alden Lake hoist. The little 37-ton engine was well liked for switching service. — MRS. L. REIL COLLECTION (LOWER LEFT) An M&NW section crew at Gipson siding about 1906. — RAY NOYES COLLECTION

Loading log cars with a Decker log loader at Camp 17 (Colbrath) on the M&NW. Empty log cars passed through the base of the loader on a special track. Note logs being rolled up for loading at the right of the scene. (RIGHT) A horse team skidding beautiful white pine logs along the Minnesota & North Wisconsin. — BOTH FRANK KING COLLECTION

floating of their logs beyond it to Cloquet. In order to construct such a sorting works, Brooks-Scanlon resorted to the courts (bringing condemnation proceedings in May 1904). In lengthy testimony, it convinced the latter that the additional expense and great loss of time in delivery involved in water transportation of logs made rail shipment imperative, and an opinion in its favor was soon handed down. Almost at the same time, the Cloquet lumbermen's objections were being rendered academic by the fact that Frederick Weyerhaeuser, the most important person on the Cloquet economic scene, had decided to extend his nearby Duluth & Northeastern Railroad from Rush Lake to Cloquet. He, too, was ready to abandon the river and resort instead to all-rail movement of logs to his mills at Cloquet.

Brooks-Scanlon also owned large stands of timber east of the Duluth & Iron Range road, and during 1902 rumors were flying concerning extension of the Minnesota & North Wisconsin. The *Duluth News Tribune* for November 28, 1902 reported:

Definite information as to plans of the Minnesota & North Wisconsin Road has been obtained, but its future after the logging industry on the line is exhausted is for time to tell.

The road now extends from Scanlon to a point about six miles from Two Harbors, but it is not the intention to extend the line to that town. The road will run northeasterly from its present eastern terminus and cross the D&IR about 12 miles above Two Harbors.

The ultimate length of the M&NW will be about 100 miles of main line. This is remarkable for a road which is built purely for logging purposes. It is of standard gauge and present equipment consists of eleven locomotives and 250 cars. The

The crew of M&NW's little 0-4-0 switcher ponder how to get her tender back on the rails. It appears that the tender was derailed during track ballasting operations. — MRS. L. RIEL COLLECTION

A happy Sunday crowd ride a blueberry picking special over the Minnesota & North Wisconsin line somewhere north of Duluth. — MRS. L. RIEL COLLECTION

A woodburning 4-4-0 No. 64 on Brooks-Scanlon's logging railroad in Florida, the Live Oak, Perry & Gulf. The road continued to burn wood in its locomotives until 1943. — FRANK KING COLLECTION

Big timber was found along the headwaters of the Sucker River near the end of the Minnesota & North Wisconsin. — FRANK KING COLLECTION

general business of the road, aside from the logging traffic, is said to be surprisingly big. Speaking of the future of the road, a railroad man said yesterday, "The M&NW seems destined to be a local line for general traffic purposes if the owners see fit to continue its operation after the timber is delivered. I have heard that if the Duluth & Northern Minnesota does not extend to the Canadian border through the Gunflint region, this line will." It is expected that the Port Arthur, Duluth & Western will extend to a connection with the Iron Range Road next year, but everything is up in the air as regards projects that will give communication between Duluth and Canadian North Shore points.

This proposed extension of the Minnesota & North Wisconsin was never built, however. Brooks-Scanlon disposed of its timber holdings in the north to other interests, and these big stands were later penetrated by the Duluth & Northern Minnesota and the General Logging Company.

Most of the timber south of the Duluth & Iron Range was gone by 1909, and the last log was cut at Scanlon in the fall of that year. One year later, the big mill was dismantled and shipped to a new Brooks-Scanlon operation in Florida. The company's sale of its timberlands in the north served to shorten its operations in Minnesota by at least a decade. It can only be concluded that the owners deliberately

Tariff covering the handling of pine saw logs over the rails of the Minnesota & North Wisconsin Railroad. —FRANK KING COLLECTION

rushed to wind up their affairs there in their eagerness to reinvest their capital in Florida, Louisiana, and Oregon timberlands. At the height of its operations in Minnesota, however, Brooks-Scanlon employed some 1,500 men. It was they who cut the record-breaking section in the state, Section 35-53-13, located near the end of the Minnesota & North Wisconsin at the headwaters of the Sucker River, which contained 33 million board feet of pine!

Between 1909 and 1912 the Minnesota & North Wisconsin was operated for Weyerhaeuser's Johnson-Wentworth Lumber Company for movement of logs to its mill at Cloquet. In 1911, 19.6 miles of line east of Alden Junction were abandoned, leaving 34.5 miles of main line to Scanlon. There were only three locomotives, 16 cars, and one caboose in use at the time. Apparently, enough cars were acquired from the Duluth & Northeastern to carry on operations during these last years. The Minnesota & North Wisconsin applied to abandon early in 1912 and received permission to do so that same year.

It was in 1886 that the town of Knife Falls was renamed Cloquet (Klo-kay), and from then until now Cloquet has remained a name synonymous with the forest products industry. The community began to grow in the early 1880's when the Knife Falls Boom Company received its charter from the state legislature. At the time, it was considered impractical to drive logs beyond the St. Louis River Dalles. By 1886, Knife Falls had become a thriving sawmilling community, strategically located on the river above the falls.

In the next few years, Duluth lumbermen acquired substantial stands of timber in the immense pine area north of Lake Superior, drained by the Cloquet and St. Louis rivers, and began thinking of

Mogul No. 291 of the M&NW pauses with her crew at Scanlon before picking up a train of empty log cars and heading north into timber. No. 291 was built by Dickson in 1882 for the Delaware, Lackawanna & Western. — MRS. L. RIEL COLLECTION

Picking up the steel rails on the M&NW north of Duluth in 1913 using a McGiffert loader. The man standing at the extreme right is A. S. Brooks, superintendent of the railroad. (RIGHT) Upon abandonment of the M&NW trestle across the St. Louis River at Scanlon in 1913, the structure was planked over for wagons and automobiles to use. — BOTH FRANK KING COLLECTION

Frederick Weyerhaeuser, North America's most prominent lumberman, was an extensive user of logging railroads in Minnesota and Wisconsin. —MINNESOTA HISTORICAL SOCIETY

driving the logs from those sites to their mills Duluth. Cloquet, however, had no intention of relinquishing its position as a milling center to Duluth, some 20 miles down river. Duluth lumbermen contested the legality of the Knife Falls boom, claiming that it decreased the worth of their timber one dollar per thousand board feet from what it would be were the river open for logs to go beyond Cloquet to Duluth. Backed by the powerful Weyerhaeuser, Cloquet lumbermen refused to give in.

Weyerhaeuser had in 1883 acquired an interest in a small Cloquet lumbering firm that later became the Cloquet Lumber Company. In 1896 he formed the Northern Lumber Company to acquire the properties of the C.N. Nelson Lumber Company at Cloquet, including the Mesabe Southern Railway, and was rapidly acquiring additional pine stumpage tributary to the Cloquet and St. Louis rivers. In 1898, to tap important pine stands in the Cloquet River Valley, some 30 miles north of Duluth, the Duluth Logging & Contracting Company began construction of a logging railroad. This road, which extended 27.5 miles from Lynds (later renamed Hornby) on the Duluth & Iron Range to Island Lake, was incorporated as the Duluth & Northeastern Railroad on September 30 of that year. Logs were railed to Island Lake, where they were dumped and floated down the Cloquet and St. Louis rivers to the mills at Cloquet. At the time, the road's headquarters, shops, and three-stall enginehouse were located at Rush Lake.

During 1899 four locomotives and 64 logging cars were available to handle an estimated 30 million board feet of timber over the Duluth & Northeastern. That year, too, the Cloquet Lumber Company acquired a two-thirds interest in the Duluth Logging & Contracting Company, which held the lease of the

Hawthorne, Nebagamon & Superior logging train somewhere in Douglas County, Wisconsin. This road, along with the Duluth & Northeastern, Mesabe Southern and the Minneapolis, St. Paul & Ashland were all part of Weyerhaeuser's little logging railroad empire in Wisconsin and Minnesota. — HOWARD PEDDLE COLLECTION

Minneapolis, St. Paul & Ashland No. 16 at the log landing near Ashland, Wisconsin. — HOWARD PEDDLE COLLECTION

Duluth & Northeastern and the logging contract. To extend branch line trackage, 255 tons of 30-pound rail were acquired from Weyerhaeuser's Nebagamon Lumber Company in nearby northern Wisconsin. Duluth & Northeastern officers in 1900 included F. Weyerhaeuser (at St. Paul), president; H.C. Hornby (of Cloquet), vice-president and general manager; and J.E. Lynds (of Cloquet), secretary and treasurer.

In the spring of 1902 water levels on the Cloquet and St. Louis rivers were not high enough to float logs downstream. Nearly 150 million board feet of them were stranded along the two rivers, awaiting sufficient rainfall to send them on their way. The Cloquet mills were forced to shut down, and their managers looked with envy at Brooks-Scanlon's round-the-clock operation at nearby Scanlon, which received its log supply entirely by rail.

Anxious to become independent of the uncertainties of log driving on the rivers, the Weyerhaeuser interests began surveying an extension of the Duluth & Northeastern from Rush Lake to Cloquet, and the directors authorized such a project in 1904. By April 1, 1904 the old line to Island Lake had been taken up, and by late summer the new line, approximately 42 miles long, was completed from Rush Lake to the St. Louis River at Cloquet. In exchange for a half interest in its logging railroad, the

Panoramic view of Upper Cloquet, taken before the 1918 fire, showing the two Northern Lumber Company sawmills. At the time, the three Weyerhaeuser lumber companies operated five sawmills in the community producing a total of 250,000,000 feet of lumber annually. — CARLTON COUNTY HISTORICAL SOCIETY (LEFT) *Big Cloquet* mill of the Cloquet Lumber Company. — E. A. KRUGER COLLECTION

Hot pond and sorting works on the St. Louis River at Cloquet. Train of logs standing along the river bank was waiting to be dumped. — MINNESOTA HISTORICAL SOCIETY

Duluth & Northeastern's little Mogul No. 2 syphons water from a spring creek near Bartlett. Such procedure was common in the woods where watertanks were nonexistent. Upon the completion of logging in the area, the temporary log trestle was disassembled, the logs being sent to the mills at Cloquet. — CARL H. HENDRICKSON, JR.

Working steam, D&NE Mogul No. 2 crosses a cribbed log bridge on the Caribou Lake Branch during 1923. The grade at this location was so steep that the little engine could pull only one loaded car up at a time. This spur extended off the Duluth, Winnipeg & Pacific near Bartlett and was isolated from the D&NE. — CARL HENDRICKSON, JR.

A 1907 scene at Saginaw looking north along the D&NE line where it crossed the Missabe Road. Note the pile of empty beer kegs alongside Saginaw House, a place where loggers slaked their thirst while waiting to change trains. Today, Saginaw is the northern terminus of the D&NE. — DM&IR HISTORICAL COLLECTION

92

D&NE Mogul No. 19 ready to pull out onto the main line with a mixed train of pulpwood and saw logs. —HOWARD PEDDLE COLLECTION

D&NE No. 1 attached to a long train of log cars awaits the "highball" signal to roll from Camp 108. — HOWARD PEDDLE COLLECTION

Mesabe Southern, the Northern Lumber Company was now given a half interest in the Duluth & Northeastern. Northern Lumber and the Mesabe Southern were also Weyerhaeuser-controlled properties.

In 1905, upon completion of a bridge over the St. Louis River, the Duluth & Northeastern entered Cloquet itself. Cost of the extension, exclusive of the bridge, was $256,177, representing an average expense per mile of $6,100. Steam-heated "hot ponds" were constructed in the river at Cloquet to enable the mills to operate in the winter — a necessity if logs were to be delivered on a year-round basis. Duluth & Northeastern shop and headquarters were moved from Rush Lake to Dunlap Island at Cloquet. A combination baggage-passenger car was procured, and passenger service was soon inaugurated. The road at this time owned four locomotives and 119 logging cars.

By 1909 the Duluth & Northeastern was doing a respectable business, handling almost 200,000 tons of freight and some 12,500 passengers. Equipment by then included nine locomotives, 182 logging cars, 92 miscellaneous freight cars, and two passenger cars.

A cleared grade for a new logging spur on the D&NE. — FRANK KING COLLECTION (RIGHT) A steel laying crew follow with the ties and rails for the new spur using No. 19 for power. — WALTER BENDER COLLECTION

The great 1918 forest fire left the D&NE enginehouse at Cloquet in a shambles. In spite of the damage sustained, most of the locomotives shown in this scene were repaired and returned to active service. — CARLTON COUNTY HISTORICAL SOCIETY

D&NE No. 1 clears the line after a storm during the winter of 1921. When the snow was deeper a flanger or plow was called on the scene. (BELOW) With the battle against the light snowfall over, the crew pose proudly for the camera. — BOTH E. A. KRUGER COLLECTION

During 1910, to reach timber on recently burned-over lands, 20 miles of new main line from Harris Lake to the Duluth & Iron Range were constructed, and the old line via Sullivan Lake was abandoned. Two years later, the road handled a record 686,276 tons of freight and 20,831 passengers. Duluth & Northeastern traffic statistics would never again attain such heights, however, and estimates of timber available beyond 1918 forecast the end of big-time sawmilling at Cloquet within a decade.

The summer of 1918 was hot and dry in northern Minnesota, and by fall the woods were tinder. On October 12 small brush fires to the west of Cloquet erupted out of control and raged down the St. Loius River Valley toward the community. At first few lumbermen took the threat of fire very seriously, and the mills continued operating. By sundown, however, the holocaust was sweeping through the great lumber piles, and ignited boards, picked up by the wind, were descending upon the town like flaming firebrands.

That night, Cloquet burned to the ground, with a staggering loss of human lives and property in the surrounding area. A total of 453 persons perished in the flames, and 85 died subsequently from serious burns. However, although the town itself was completely destroyed, only four of its 9,000 inhabitants were killed in the fire. Without doubt the human loss would have been far greater had not the Great Northern station agent Lawrence Farley, on his own authority, packed every available empty freight car in Cloquet with human cargo and dispatched them all to safety.

Ultimately, the town rose like a Phoenix from the ashes. The eagerness of its people to rebuild so motivated the Weyerhaeuser interests that they joined in the movement, in spite of the short-term future for the lumbering industry there. Actually, diversification into new forest products, along with the continued expansion of the Northwest Paper Company, was to assure Cloquet of a bright future.

View of General Logging Company's headquarters at Cascade, 131 miles from Cloquet. — FRANK KING COLLECTION

The last chapter on big-time railroad logging in Minnesota was still to be written. The General Logging Company, which conducted logging activities for the Cloquet Lumber Company and the Northern Lumber Company, developed elaborate plans for logging the state's most northerly regions. In 1927 and 1928 it ran an extension from Cascade Junction on the Duluth & Northeastern into Lake and Cook counties. Fifty-one miles of new line were constructed, connecting with the recently abandoned Duluth & Northern Minnesota Railway near mile post 73. The main line of the D&NM was used for the next 24 miles to Cascade, where a four-stall enginehouse and coaling and watering facilities were built. Beyond Cascade, General Logging constructed 36 miles of new line to Clearwater and Rose lakes on the Canadian border. Most of the rail for this extension was obtained from the abandoned line of the Duluth & Northern Minnesota between Knife River and mile post 69.5.

General Logging's three-truck Heisler No. 81 spots cars for loading and begins to make up a train of loads in northernmost Minnesota during the winter of 1929-1930. — E. A. KRUGER COLLECTION

Duluth & Northeastern crews had operating rights over the General Logging Company line from Cascade Junction to Cascade, and handled all road work between Cascade and Cloquet — a distance of 131 miles. General Logging Company crews and locomotives performed all work east of Cascade. The line between Cascade and Cloquet was a busy section of railroad during the winter months, and an examination of train dispatchers' sheets for February 1930 shows as many as 12 trains daily in each direction. Nine locomotives graced the General Logging

Husky, low-drivered Cambria & Indiana No. 7 became General Logging Company No. 90 — P. E. PERCY COLLECTION (LEFT) Loading cars along the General Logging Company lines in Cook County during 1929 with a Clyde Decker loader. — E. A. KRUGER COLLECTION

A fire going in the cook shack seems to be the only activity at General Logging Company's Camp 3. The scene is at Brule Lake north of Cascade. — E. A. KRUGER COLLECTION

The many hollow centered logs contained in this carload, coupled with the long rail haul to Cloquet, quite well sums up why the General Logging Company operations in Cook County was not a financial success. — E. A. KRUGER COLLECTION

Company roster, including two husky ex-Cambria & Indiana Mikados, the largest engines ever used on a Minnesota logging railroad.

Most of the marketable timber along General Logging's lines had been removed by 1938. Since much of the timber in this area was of inferior quality, the total operation was somewhat of a disappointment monetarily. With the removal of General Logging's lines durings 1939, there remained little reason for the Duluth & Northeastern to maintain its road between Saginaw and Hornby. In 1941 permission was granted to abandon the 46 miles of track, leaving only the 11.4 miles of main line between Saginaw (on the Duluth, Missabe & Iron Range) and Cloquet.

In 1929 control of the Duluth & Northeastern had passed from the Cloquet Lumber Company and the Northern Lumber Company to the Northwest Paper Company. The last change in ownership occurred in 1963, when Northwest Paper was sold to Potlatch Forests, Inc., of San Francisco.

The Duluth & Northeastern continues to provide freight service six days per week between Cloquet and the Duluth, Missabe & Iron Range connection at Saginaw, as well as to perform switching services for forest products industries in Cloquet. Still operating under its original name and charter, it represents the final remnant of the vast network of logging railroads which once covered much of northern Minnesota.

Modern day train crew pose with their 1,000 hp Electro-Motive diesel switcher No. 35, the Duluth & Northeastern's newest locomotive. — D&NE PHOTO

Drifting downgrade from Saginaw, D&NE No. 28 heads toward Cloquet with carloads of pulpwood and other commodities for local industries. This engine is former DM&IR No. 332 and is now on exhibit at the Lake Superior Museum of Transportation and Industry at Duluth. — FRANK KING

D&NE No. 14 drifts by namesake Northeastern Hotel in Cloquet. (LEFT) No. 16 eases downgrade across State Highway No. 33 with coal and pulpwood for the forest products industries at Cloquet. — BOTH FRANK KING

The Lima Locomotive Works built 0-6-0 type switcher No. 29 which was the newest steam locomotive on the Duluth & Northeastern. She was constructed in 1944 for the U.S. War Department. — FRANK KING

Slide-valved Duluth & Northeastern Consolidation No. 16 drifts by former Duluth & Iron Range caboose No. 04. — JIM SHAUGHNESSY (BELOW) A winter scene on the D&NE with No. 14 blasting upgrade near Saginaw. — FRANK KING

Duluth & Northeastern No. 14 switches between the huge pulpwood piles at the Northwest Paper Company in Cloquet. — WILLIAM D. MIDDLETON (LEFT) Consolidation No. 27 undergoes repairs in the company shops at Cloquet. — FRANK KING

DULUTH & NORTHEASTERN R. R. CO.

1/2 fare

GOOD FOR ONE FIRST CLASS PASSAGE
CLOQUET, MINN.

TO *Saginaw + return*

WHEN OFFICIALLY STAMPED
GOOD ONLY ONE DAY FROM DATE OF SALE AS STAMPED
ON BACK HEREOF

Void if Showing any Alterations.
NOT TRANSFERABLE

FORM
B | 14202

Gen'l | Pass'r Ag't.

A long drag freight, with No. 27 on the point, drifts into Saginaw with cars to be interchanged with the Duluth, Missabe & Iron Range at Saginaw. — FRANK KING

D&NE steamer No. 14 takes water from an ice-festooned water tank near the company's headquarters and one-time station in Cloquet. (BELOW) An early morning freight bound for Saginaw crosses highway No. 33 and throws up a lot of loose snow on this cold winters day.

— BOTH WILLIAM D. MIDDLETON

Old man winter creates additional work on the railroad. Switches must be cleaned constantly to avoid derailments. In this scene, a log train on the Duluth & Iron Range Rail Road's Eastern Mesaba Branch during the winter of 1913. Consolidation No. 49 was built for the road by the Baldwin Locomotive Works in 1888. — FRANK KING COLLECTION

5

ALONG THE IRON RANGE

Because their timber holdings were situated on lands containing iron, a number of Minnesota lumbermen fell heir to vast fortunes. Among there were W.C. Yawkey, William Sauntry, and C.N. Nelson. Yawkey, a lumberman from Detroit, had the good fortune of owning 80 acres of ore lands north of Virgina that contained between five and ten million tons of iron, for which the American Steel & Wire Company agreed to pay him royalties of 15 cents per ton. Since the pine alone netted him a handsome profit, the added royalties were pure icing on the cake. William Sauntry, of Stillwater, received some $750,000 from the same company for his adjacent property, which he had bought back from the state, after the pine had been removed, by paying $5,000 in taxes. This land had originally belonged to the Weyerhaeuser combination.

C.N. Nelson, who got his start in lumbering at Stillwater during the 1870's, owned substantial timberland along the Mesabi Range between Kinney and Virginia. A Cloquet lumberman since 1880, he had first logged near the St. Louis River a few miles upstream from that communtiy. During 1890, to reach timber some ten miles from the river, he had constructed a logging railroad starting from a point near Gowan on the Duluth & Winnipeg Railway.

Logs were hauled to a landing on the river and floated to his mill at Cloquet.

Access to timber along the Mesabi Range also required a logging railroad, and Nelson incorporated the Mesabe Southern Railway Company on January 27, 1894 with a capitalization of $40,000. The road, nicknamed the "Smokey Southern," extended 33 miles from the St. Louis River in Township 56-18, where logs were dumped and floated to Cloquet, and to Erwin. Later, branches from Haywire Junction to Klondike (4 miles) and from Section House 2 to Dorsey (3 miles) brought the total mileage to 40. The lines were laid with an astonishing conglomeration of secondhand rails, weighing from 30, 40, 45, 50, 56, to 60 pounds per yard!

Discovery of large iron ore deposits on Nelson's timberlands near Virginia prompted the Illinois Steel Company to negotiate acquisition of his mineral rights. Nelson, in poor health, wanted to retire from business and was determined to dispose of all his properties. These consisted — in addition to the ore — of 600 million board feet of pine, two sawmills in Cloquet, and his Mesabe Southern Railway. The steel company, however, desiring only the mineral rights, had expressed no interest in acquiring anything else.

Actually, Illinois Steel hoped to persuade Weyerhaeuser to buy Nelson's pine and sawmills and remove the timber overlying the ore bodies. The up-shot of all this was the formation, by Weyerhaeuser in 1896, of a new corporation, the Northern Lumber Company, through which he purchased Nelson's interests, including the Mesabe Southern, for $1,900,000. Nelson himself incorporated his mineral rights as the Northern Development Company, which he sold to Illinois Steel. Mining on the property was to begin during the late 1890's, upon Northern Lumber Company's removal of the pine. It was through these transactions that Weyerhaeuser be-came the dominant figure in Cloquet lumbering, con-trolling four of the five mills at that location.

During 1900 the Moon and Kerr mill at Vir-ginia was destroyed by fire and Weyerhaeuser ac-quired their holdings north of Virginia a short time later. By fall of 1904 some 300 men were en-gaged in extending the Mesabe Southern easterly toward the mining town of McKinley. A new logging headquarters camp, providing accommodations for approximately 500 men, was constructed about 4.5 miles northwest of Virginia. Other facilities at this location included a four-stall enginehouse and a large warehouse.

Mining closely followed the logger on the Mesabi Range. Steam shovel No. 1078 prepares to remove the stump-covered overburden from the ore body at the Hill Mine in 1908. — ITASCA COUNTY HISTORICAL SOCIETY

Banker and lumberman, Charles N. Nelson, became a multi-millionaire upon disposing of his pine and sawmill holdings to Weyerhaeuser and the iron ore to Illinois Steel. — MINNESOTA HISTORICAL SOCIETY

Mesabe Southern trains dumped their logs at this landing located along the St. Louis River south of the iron country. The logs were then floated down the river for the remainder of their journey to the mills at Cloquet. — PAUL D. SILLIMAN COLLECTION

At the height of logging operations, the Mesabe Southern's equipment consisted of six locomotives, 175 logging cars, and two cabooses. One of the engines was a small Shay acquired from Nelson's original operation at Gowan. When the Mesabe Southern ceased operation in 1912, this locomotive, along with others, went to the Duluth & Northeastern at Cloquet.

East of Virginia along the iron country a number of small logging railroad operations existed. The earliest of these, the Tower Logging Railway Company, was incorporated in 1895 with an all-encompassing objective:

> to build and operate a logging railroad, logging and transporting logs, lumbering, buying and selling pine and other lumbering lands, merchandising, and all other business naturally auxiliary to these . . .

The Tower Logging Railway connected with the Duluth & Iron Range Railroad at Murray, a short distance east of Tower. From 1895 to 1899 it performed contract logging for the Howe Lumber Company at Tower. Between Murray and Tower log cars were handled over the Duluth & Iron Range. In 1899 the company decided to go into the lumbering business itself, acquired an old sawmill in Wisconsin, and set it up at Bear Head Lake on its own line.

In 1901 the entire property of the Tower Logging Railway Company was purchased by the Tower Lumber Company, which had acquired the Howe

Mesabe Southern No. 1 spots DM&N cars for loading north of Mountain Iron. The ancient 4-4-0 type was used earlier on C. N. Nelson's logging railroad near Gowan. — ST. LOUIS COUNTY HISTORICAL SOCIETY

Mesabe Southern Mogul No. 5 switches log cars in the woods. The loader at the left appears to be a homemade contraption — MINNESOTA HISTORICAL SOCIETY

This Russel Wheel & Foundry Company advertisement featured both their seven-yard stripping car, which was popular on the Mesabi Range during the early 1900's. Mesabe Southern log car No. 99 is shown as an example of Russel Log Cars. — PAUL SILLIMAN COLLECTION

Admirers of Swallow & Hopkins *Two Spot* lend a festive mood to this scene at the Fall Lake landing during 1914. A Consolidation of unknown origin, this engine was used on the line which ran north from Fall Lake. — ROBERT HILL COLLECTION

Lumber Company millsite and timber holdings two years before. Included in the $225,000 sale were 20 miles of railroad, three locomotives, 100 logging cars, and the single-band mill at Bear Head Lake. The following year, logs began arriving at the Tower mill by both water and rail. By then there were 25 miles of railroad, four locomotives (two of them Shays), 140 logging cars, a steam log loader, and a steam shovel. The 25 miles of trackage included the 2.5 mile portage railroad between Pine Lake and Lake Vermilion, which operated with one saddle-tank locomotive plus a handful of cars.

With an annual cut of 30 million board feet, timber reserves in the Bear Head Lake area were depleted by 1905, and those at Pine Lake ran out the following year. The mill at Tower was sold to Alger-Smith in 1909 and operated by that company until 1911, when it was sold to Cook and Ketcham and began functioning as the Trout Lake Lumber Company, operating a three-mile portage railroad between Lake Vermilion and Elbow Lake.

Twenty miles east of Tower, the Swallow & Hopkins Lumber Company operated an unusual logging railroad. During the winter of 1898-99 logging operations began in the Fall Lake-Basswood Lake area about ten miles east of Winton which was the end of the Duluth & Iron Range. Two camps were built, one on Ella Hall Lake and the other on nearby Mud Lake.

The original plan called for a two-mile portage railroad from Ella Hall and Mud lakes to Fall Lake, powered by a steam operated cable haul system. From this point the logs would be floated approximately six miles to the mill at Winton. Before construction of the railroad began, however, Logging Superintendent G.H. Good decided that a locomotive-operated railway would be preferable and discarded the cable-haul plan. A small secondhand Shay was procured for motive power. Affectionately known as the *The 3 Spot*, she was the company's sole engine until 1901, when the original railroad was extended approximately three miles to Basswood Lake. By then logging in the Mud Lake-Ella Hall Lake area was completed, and that portion of the railway extending to the hoists on the lakes was removed.

Log traffic over the new four-mile portage railroad soon overtaxed the capacity of the Shay, and during 1901 a second locomotive arrived on the scene. Called *The 4 Spot*, this 35-ton Brooks Mogul was acquired from the Split Rock Lumber Company, which had found the engine unsuited to operation on its 4-½ percent grade and replaced her with a Climax-geared locomotive. *The 4 Spot* had been built in 1894 as engine No. 4 for the Cranberry Lumber Company, Ltd. of Wisconsin. The snappy little Mogul was assigned to handling trains consisting of ten

The above Mogul locomotive named the *Sally Hicks* was built by Brooks in 1894 for the Cranberry Lumber Company (Ltd.), which operated in Wisconsin along the south shore of Lake Superior. The engine was acquired by Swallow & Hopkins Lumber Company in 1901. — ALCO HISTORIC PHOTOS (LEFT) Lumberman Arthur Swallow and friends pose on the pilot beam of the former *Sally Hicks* at Fall Lake on the Four Mile Portage Railroad in 1905. — LEE BROWNELL COLLECTION

Russel logging cars across the four-mile portage, while the Shay performed spotting service at the hoist on Basswood Lake. Al Oakes was the regular engineer on *The 4 Spot* for the log haul. A friendly and helpful person, he would never pass up anyone going across the portage, often picking up a whole family of Indians and giving squaw, papoose, and older children a ride on the bunks of the Russel cars. The two locomotives were converted to burn wood, inasmuch as it was plentiful along the line. Spruce, pine, tamarack, poplar, and birch were all used for fuel. By the time the railroad ceased operations, the wood supply was just about depleted.

The Russel cars came equipped with standard bunks, consisting of heavy cross timbers placed directly above each set of trucks, and logs were secured to the bunks with chains. Conventional "corner-bind" chains were used to hold outside key logs, and "wrapper" chains employed to hold together several tiers of logs making up a full load. This tie-down

The train crew appear to be preoccupied with a problem below the cab of No. 4 as logs are being dumped into Fall Lake. — LEE BROWNELL COLLECTION

method was soon simplified by installation of "automatic car stakes," patented by Logging Superintendent Good and Al Cross, mechanical engineer for Swallow & Hopkins.

The portage railroad operated from the time the ice broke up in the spring until the lakes froze in the fall. All actual logging operations were carried on during the winter, including skidding and sleigh hauling of logs to the lakes for subsequent towing during the summer.

With its fleet of steam tugs for towing logs across the lakes, the portage railway, and the ingenious hoisting system for loading cars at Basswood Lake, the entire Swallow & Hopkins operation was unique. In the beginning, a standard log "jammer" was used to load cars; but this was later replaced by two endless chains with spikes attached, mounted on a frame, about ten feet apart, with a steam-driven mechanism providing continuous movement of logs from the water onto the cars. Another interesting aspect of the operation involved the large scows used in moving material and supplies on Fall and Basswood lakes. The scows, 30 feet wide by 80 feet long, had rails spiked to standard gauge width on their decks, making it possible to load two Russel log cars or one standard freight car on board. By using barges it was possible to roll a carload of freight off the end of the Duluth & Iron Range dock at Winton and tow it across Fall Lake to the four-mile railroad portage, where it would be moved by locomotive to Basswood Lake and placed upon another barge for movement to Prairie Portage. At Prairie Portage, the car would be pulled off the barge and across the rail portage to Prairie Portage Dam Landing by means of a block and tackle attached at the upper end and a return cable to the steam-powered launch or tug on Basswood Lake.

The portage railway hauled approximately 350 million board feet of sawlogs for Swallow & Hopkins between 1901 and 1911. In the latter year it was sold to the Hines-controlled St. Croix Lumber & Manufacturing Company, which also had a mill at Winton. The new owners continued using the line until 1920, when their mill ceased operation.

The steam log hauling engine, because of its slow speed and limited winter service, was never a serious contender to the logging railroad. The particular machine in this advertisement saw service in Tower Lumber company operations. — HOWARD PEDDLE COLLECTION

Edward Hines and Frederick Weyerhaeuser, two of the greatest names in the history of American lumbering, stand alongside each other to the far left on the observation platform of a Northern Pacific business car at Winton, Minnesota. — MINNESOTA HISTORICAL SOCIETY (LEFT) St. Croix Lumber & Manufacturing Company mill at Winton was operated by Edward Hines. — PAUL SILLIMAN COLLECTION

The St. Croix Lumber & Manufacturing Company *Brown Six* with a sleigh load of hay for the camps. — FRANK KING COLLECTION

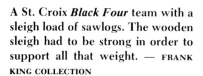

A St. Croix *Black Four* team with a sleigh load of sawlogs. The wooden sleigh had to be strong in order to support all that weight. — FRANK KING COLLECTION

A steam hauler belonging to the St. Croix Lumber firm with a train of logging sleighs. A steam hauler could handle six to eight sleighs on a good road. — FRANK KING COLLECTION

In 1909 Swallow & Hopkins began construction of another logging railroad. This line, which connected with the Duluth & Iron Range just west of Winton, extended some 20 miles north into heavy pine stands. A fleet of four new Lima Shays kept logs moving from the woods to the landing at Fall Lake. The mill operated at a reduced capacity after World War I, and it was sold to the Cloquet Lumber Company in 1922. Cloquet continued to use the Swallow & Hopkins logging railroad until 1937, when it was removed.

Duluth & Iron Range No. 49 with a log train on the Eastern Mesaba Branch. The engineer in his cab is waiting for the "highball" to proceed. (BELOW) A southbound local freight, headed by a 4-8-0 type locomotive, is about to leave the timber loading operations at D&IR Milepost 86 after picking up several cars of loads. — BOTH JACK CARR COLLECTION

In addition to sawlogs, pulpwood and ties were also important forest products in northern Minnesota. Sometimes, even stock cars were pressed into service for hauling pulpwood. — JACK CARR COLLECTION (LOWER LEFT) The odd black item was called a *hickey*. It was used by brakemen to set brakes on logging cars not equipped with standard brake wheels. The *hickey* illustrated here now belongs to the author. It was found by Howard Peddle on a logging railroad grade in northern Wisconsin.

A steam log hauler, presumably belonging to the Skibo Timber Company, with a train of loaded logging sleighs. The man seated in front steered the machine by turning the runners. The engineer/fireman in the cab worked the throttle and fed the firebox to keep the boiler hot. — FRANK KING COLLECTION

The crew of N. B. Shank Company's little *One Spot* have their picture taken before heading north to the Duluth & Iron Range interchange. This mixed consist includes both sawlogs and pulpwood. — FRANK KING COLLECTION

Twenty miles to the west, the N.B. Shank Company of Biwabik operated an 18-mile logging railroad complex, connecting with the old Duluth & Iron Range Summit Line at mile post X-14 near Biwabik. Construction began in the fall of 1909 on the line to Headquarters Camp at Silver Lake. By 1912 branches had been extended to Lost Lake and on to the St. Louis River. The company also operated a ten-mile logging line running northeasterly from the Duluth & Iron Range main line at mile post 68.5. Motive power for the Shank operation at Silver Lake consisted of two saddle-tank four-wheel switchers acquired from nearby Biwabik Mining Company. All rolling stock was supplied by the Duluth & Iron Range.

The N.B. Shank Company employed some 150 men, and most of its logging was accomplished during the winter months. A logging rate of around 60 forties per winter produced 25 to 30 carloads of logs per day. To move them to the Duluth & Iron Range interchange, two round trips (trains normally ran at night) were made daily. In 1915 N.B. Shank Company sold the line to a local logger named Jack Saari. The latter continued to log in the area until 1925, at which time the rails were removed.

Along the western Mesabi, the Powers & Simpson Logging Company, which held large logging contracts, operated a 22-mile logging railroad. Called the Duluth, Missabe & Western, it was constructed during 1898 and extended from Barclay Junction on the Great Northern near Chisholm to the log landing at Crooked Lake. In addition to the main line, there were some 10 to 12 miles of branches in operation at all times. Equipment consisted of three locomotives and 82 logging cars. Logger George Simpson was president of the road, and A.H. (Al) Powers was vice-president.

Logs were floated from Crooked Lake down the Prairie River into the Mississippi, to sawmills at Minneapolis and Dubuque, Iowa. Logging operations

Locomotive No. 2 of the N. B. Shank Lumber Company is having her saddle tank filled by the syphoning water system. The water is sucked through the pipes from a nearby lake. This little 0-4-0 was constructed by the Pittsburgh Locomotive Works in the 1890's for the Biwabik Mining Company. — D. B. SHANK COLLECTION

lasted until 1908, and the road was dismantled shortly thereafter. That same year, Al Powers moved to Coos County in Oregon, taking his rails with him. Rolled in Germany in 1878, they had been used on the Minneapolis & St. Louis for 18 years before they went to the Powers & Simpson road. When they were finally pulled up on the Smith-Powers logging line in Oregon during the 1920's, they had seen a half century of rugged service.

Al Powers was an avid sportsman, interested in horse racing, baseball, and prize fighting. During the summer of 1901, when reformers succeeded in prohibiting exhibition of a prize fight in Hibbing, he met the challenge head-on by ordering a train of logging flats made up. A good part of the town climbed aboard and was taken into nearby Itasca County, where the fight took place.

This writer's father, George R. King, recalls conditions on the Duluth, Missabe & Western, a typical Minnesota logging railroad at the turn of the century:

My first railroad job was in 1900 on the old Powers and Simpson logging road. I was helping to load logs at a camp on the line, about four or five miles from Crooked Lake, when Conductor Paddy Hines asked me one day if I'd care to go braking on the road and, of course, I jumped at the chance. Only an inexperienced man would have accepted such a job on an outfit like the Powers and Simpson. There were link and pin couplings, no air brakes on the train —

Ten-Wheeler No. 3 of the Duluth, Missabe & Western syphons water at the Stone Lake log hoist north of Hibbing. This process took much more time than the taking of water directly from a water tank. — MINNESOTA HISTORICAL SOCIETY

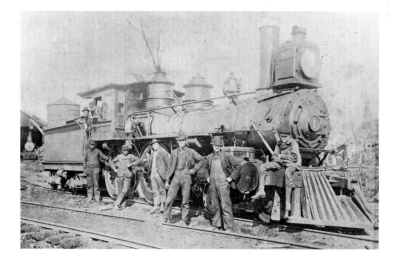

Duluth, Missabe & Western's locomotive No. 1 at the headquarters of Powers & Simpson near Hibbing. The fourth man from the left in this scene is Al Powers, vice-president of the company. — GEORGE B. ABDILL COLLECTION

A breathtaking view of Power & Simpson's huge log rollway at Crooked Lake around the turn of the century. Before the winter was over approximately 40 million feet of logs were piled here. Duluth, Missabe & Western No. 3 has just brought in a train of logs to add to the pile. — HIBBING HISTORICAL SOCIETY

A Decker loader loads Russel log cars at a Powers & Simpson camp. Safety was not a prime consideration at this time judging from the top loader standing on a log about to be placed on a car. — HIBBING HISTORICAL SOCIETY

Flamboyant logger, Al Powers, with his two race horses. — HIBBING HISTORICAL SOCIETY

only the engine was equipped with air. Time and one-half, the sixteen-hour law, etc., were at that time unheard of. If we went out to pick up a train of logs and had trouble along the way, we worked until we got the loads back to the landing at Crooked Lake. It made no difference if we didn't get back until the next day — we were expected to work right through. We were paid by the month, brakemen getting around $35. The logs were held on the cars by chains — corner binds and wrappers. Each car was equipped with several feet of logging chain. The standard log was 16 feet long — others being 12 and 14 feet . . . Brakemen carried a "hickey," an iron crank which had a square end that fitted into a socket on the brake shaft. Nobody set up many brakes because it only meant that you would have to stay out there and release them all afterwards. When coupling up the cars, one had to be extremely careful, especially at night, for quite often the logs would overhang the ends of the cars and would practically touch when the cars came together.

117

The first passenger train crossed the new Rainy River bridge during April of 1908, establishing through service between Virginia and Fort Frances, Ontario, Canada, via the Duluth, Rainy Lake & Winnipeg Railway. At the head end of this passenger train was DLR&W No. 3 which later became Virginia & Rainy Lake Company No. 3. — FRANK KING COLLECTION

6

RAINY LAKE COUNTRY

As the twentieth century opened, lumbermen turned their attention to the largest white pine stand remaining in the Lake States, several billion board feet of timber extending north of the Mesabi Range to Rainy River on the Canadian border. Wirt H. Cook and William O'Brien, who owned sizable timber holdings in the Sand Lake county some 20 miles northwest of Virginia, formed the Minnesota Land & Construction Company to conduct their logging and railroad-building operations and built a new mill in Virginia at Silver Lake (on the site of the burned down Moon and Kerr mill).

On August 15, 1901 the two lumbermen chartered the Duluth, Virginia & Rainy Lake Railway to move their timber from the woods into Virginia. The Duluth, Virginia & Rainy Lake main line extended to Lake Junction (later renamed Britt), ten miles north of Virginia, from which point the Sand Lake line was eventually constructed to Sturgeon Lake, some 20 miles west. By 1903 six large Mogul-type locomotives acquired from the Dickson Manufacturing Company for road service and two small Porter Moguls for woods work made up the motive power roster.

On May 1, 1905, to facilitate acquisition of additional timber holdings and extension of the railroad toward the Canadian border, the Virginia &

Rainy Lake Company was incorporated — with capitalization of $2,000,000 — as a holding company for the stock of the railway construction and associated logging activities. That same year the railway reached Ashawa, another 18 miles nearer Canada.

Significant events that would shape the destiny of the railroad had been taking place in Canada. In 1899 the Canadian Northern had been formed to compete with the Canadian Pacific across Canada's prairie region. In assembling this system Canadian railroad builders Mackenzie and Mann had acquired the Minnesota & Manitoba Railroad, which dipped south of Lake of the Woods through Minnesota, providing the Canadian Northern with a through line between Winnipeg and the Canadian lakehead. By 1902 the Canadian Northern represented a 1,285-mile network, and its directors were keeping careful track of progress on the logging railroad that was working its way north toward the border.

Before the end of 1905 Mackenzie, Mann and Company acquired Cook and O'Brien's interest in the Duluth, Virginia & Rainy Lake, and control of the road passed to Montreal. The name of the road was changed to the Duluth, Rainy Lake & Winnipeg at that time. Access to Duluth's extensive port facilities

A view along the Duluth, Winnipeg & Pacific at Cook. The enclosed water tank exhibits the Canadian influence on the road. (LEFT) Roller-coaster trackage on one of the many Virginia & Rainy Lake Company logging spurs. — BOTH ST. LOUIS COUNTY HISTORICAL SOCIETY

and rail connections was of topmost priority, and the new proprietors moved immediately to close the 66-mile gap between Fort Frances, Ontario and Cook, Minnesota. One of the more important conditions of sale of the railway to the Canadian Northern was that the former would furnish the rail required by Cook and O'Brien to carry on their logging operations.

Other conditions of sale designed to protect the lumber company were as follows:

That cars be promptly furnished as required by the lumber company and handled by the railway (Duluth, Rainy Lake & Winnipeg) so as not to unduly delay the operations of the lumber company; and that the log trains of the lumber company be given the right-of-way over all except passenger trains and time freight trains.

When lumber camp outfits and logging spurs require moving from one part of the railway to another, the railway agrees to permit the lumber company to do so under its own motive power at the rate of 50 cents per train mile to be paid to the railway.

In the event of the lumber company requiring to send their locomotives under steam or otherwise over the line of the railway for repairs, the railway agrees to permit this service, subject to the usual conditions referred to in the "Official Classification" from time to time.

Any repair work on locomotives or cars preformed by the railway for the lumber company shall be on the basis of cost plus 10 percent for both labor and supplies.

That water for engines be furnished from tanks of either the railway or the lumber company to the other without charge.

This station is Britt, the junction between the original V&RL line with the main line of the Duluth, Virginia & Rainy Lake road. — DW&P COLLECTION (BELOW) Dickson-built Mogul No. 11 in 1902. She was sold to the Minnesota & North Wisconsin in 1906 where she continued to haul logs. — ALCO HISTORIC PHOTOS

By 1907 rails had reached Glendale, 16 miles north of Cook. The next year witnessed completion of 49 miles of road to Ranier, opposite Fort Frances on Rainy River. In April 1908 the first passenger train crossed the Rainy River bridge, establishing through service over the Duluth, Rainy Lake & Winnipeg between Virgina and Fort Frances. South of Virginia, the Duluth, Missabe & Northern provided the link into Duluth.

Mackenzie and Mann continued their efforts to extend their railroad into Duluth, and on March 18, 1909 they incorporated the Duluth, Winnipeg & Pacific Railroad to build such a line. During 1912 the Duluth, Rainy Lake & Winnipeg was leased to the Duluth, Winnipeg & Pacific *Railway*, which also leased the physical plant of the Duluth, Winnipeg & Pacific *Railroad*; but the Canadian Northern continued to control the operation through its ownership of a majority of the capital stock.

Lumber from the Virginia & Rainy Lake mill at Virginia was to constitute the major commodity handled over this new Duluth, Winnipeg & Pacific line. Virginia & Rainy Lake had a dock at Duluth from which lumber by the shipload was sent to the lower lakes. Further, large quantities of lumber were interchanged at Duluth-Superior for movement throughout the Midwest. Earlier ideas of participating in the rapidly growing ore traffic from the Mesabi Range failed to materialize.

During World War I the Duluth, Winnipeg & Pacific, along with the Canadian Northern, fell upon hard times. The over-extended and insolvent roads passed into the control of the Canadian Government Railway, subsequently to become part of the Canadian National Railways System. The Duluth, Winnipeg & Pacific later formed a part of the Grand Trunk Corporation, a wholly-owned subsidiary of

Husky Duluth, Winnipeg & Pacific No. 2464 makes a
run for the grade over the Laurentian Divide just north
of Virginia during 1953. Today diesel power handles
the consists, with as much as 15,000 horsepower on the
point, making easy work of the grades over which the
little logging trains struggled three-quarters of a century
ago. — FRANK KING (RIGHT) A letter from the Virginia
& Rainy Lake Company to the DW&P requesting
additional rail for logging operations. — DW&P
COLLECTION

"THE LARGEST, MOST MODERN AND COMPLETE WHITE PINE LUMBER PLANT IN THE WO!

The stacking crew unload slabs of thick clear whi
into the stacking yard. The Virginia & Rainy Lak
of this grade lumber at all times. (RIGHT) Four
showing the two large sawmills and a portion of

DAILY CAPACITY,

ANI

pine off the sawmill tramway which ran
Company carried millions of board feet
abs of clear white pine. (LEFT) A view
he log dock and lake at Virginia. — ALL

WO MILLS, ONE MILLION FEET

UAL CAPACITY, THREE HUNDRED MILLION FEET.

At the right, a portion of the mill pond and mill No. 3. — HOWARD PEDDLE COLLECTION (BELOW) Panoramic view showing the mill facilities and general offices of the Virginia & Rainy Lake Company at Virginia, Minnesota. — FRANK KING COLLECTION

EDWARD HINES, PRESIDENT
WILLIAM O'BRIEN, VICE PRESIDENT
H. C. HORNBY, SECRETARY
F. E. WEYERHAEUSER, TREASURER
THOS. S. WHITTEN, GEN'L MANAGER
FRED N. TAYLOR, SALES MANAGER
C. H. ROGERS, SUPT. OF MILLS

MANUFACTURING PLANT AND GENERAL OFFICES OF
THE VIRGINIA & RAINY LAKE COMPANY, VIRGINIA, MINNESOTA.

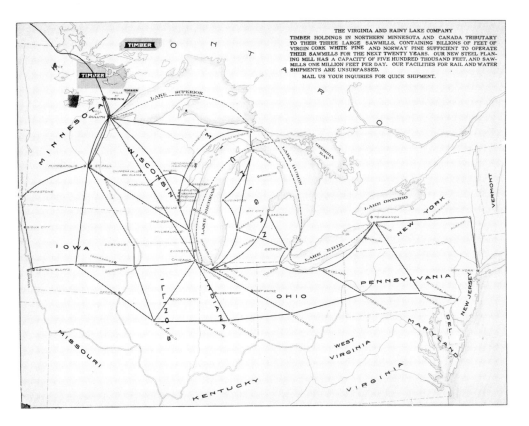

Virginia & Rainy Lake Company map showing timber holdings and lumber distribution routes. — FRANK KING COLLECTION (BELOW) Postcard view showing V&RL sawmill complex at Virginia, Minnesota. — PETE BONESTEEL COLLECTION

The Virginia & Rainy Lake Co.   Virginia, Minnesota.   The World's Largest Manufacturers of White Pine Lumber.   View showing two large Saw Mills, Main Power Plant and Portion of Log Pond.

Canadian National. Today's Duluth, Winnipeg & Pacific constitutes an extremely vital link between Western Canada and the Midwest, bearing little resemblance to its parent logging railroad, the Duluth, Virginia & Rainy Lake, founded three-quarters of a century ago by Cook and O'Brien. Nevertheless, lumber continues to be a major commodity handled over the road, though it now moves all the way from the mills in British Columbia.

At the time of the sale of the Duluth, Rainy Lake & Winnipeg to the Canadian Northern, Chicago lumberman Edward Hines was already formulating bold plans for a giant new combine to log the vast pine stand that the logging railroad had made accessible. In December 1908 Hines, Cook, O'Brien, and Weyerhaeuser, all owners of huge timber holdings, pooled their resources in the Virginia & Rainy Lake Company. Capitalized at

$10,700,000, there had never been a logging and lumbering operation in Minnesota or anywhere else in the Lake States to compare with it. The sawmill complex on Silver Lake in Virginia was expanded to produce 1 million board feet of lumber per day, and the company proudly acclaimed it the world's largest white pine plant. By that time traffic over the new road required the services of six large Moguls, three Consolidations, and two Ten-Wheelers.

One year later the Virginia & Rainy Lake Company acquired, for the sum of $1,500,000, an estimated 200 million board feet of white pine in Cook County, 14 miles north of Two Harbors. Some 20 miles of spurs were constructed off Alger-Smith's Duluth & Northern Minnesota Railway, near the Gooseberry River, into the Virginia & Rainy Lake timber. In places the old Nestor grade, from which the rails had recently been removed, was used. Vir-

123

LOCOMOTIVES OF THE
VIRGINIA & RAINY LAKE COMPANY

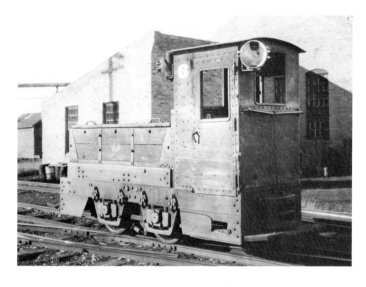

Two-truck Shay No. 20 was built by the Lima Locomotive Works for the Minnesota Land & Construction Company, a predecessor of V&RL, during 1903. — PEDERSON'S PHOTO STUDIO — FRANK KING COLLECTION

Battery-operated electric motor No. 6 was one of several used to distribute lumber from the mill to curing piles. They operated over a system of 17 miles of narrow-gauge tramways at the mill. — PEDERSON'S PHOTO STUDIO — FRANK KING COLLECTION

Shay No. 21 was also built for the Minnesota Land & Construction company during 1903. She and subsequent V&RL Shays Nos. 22, 23, and 24 were three-truck models. — PEDERSON'S PHOTO STUDIO — FRANK KING COLLECTION

Baldwin-built Consolidation No. 17 spent her latter years switching the Virginia Mill. (BELOW) No. 3 was built by Porter for the DV&RL in 1906. The 45-ton Mogul, along with sisters Nos. 1 and 2, spent most of their time working branches and spurs. — BOTH PEDERSON'S PHOTO STUDIO — FRANK KING COLLECTION

ginia & Rainy Lake locomotives (Consolidation No. 19 and Shays No. 21 and No. 22) and crews moved logs over their lines to the Duluth & Northern Minnesota. The logs were cut at the Virginia & Rainy Lake mill at Duluth, acquired some years before from the Lesure Lumber Company.

From 1905 to 1911 the main Virginia & Rainy Lake operations north of Virginia were located west of Sand Lake. Headquarters for the district was at Camp 35 near the shores of Clear Lake. By 1909 Virginia & Rainy Lake motive power consisted of three small Moguls, five Consolidations, and five Shays. In addition the company owned 200 Russel logging cars and three steam jammers for loading. It acquired from the Canadian Northern enough steel to build railroads into its vast holdings, connecting at the main line of the Duluth, Rainy Lake & Winnipeg at Britt, Cusson, Arbutus, and Kinmount. The length of the logging lines totaled about 150 miles at any given time, although the lines themselves varied from year to year.

In 1912 Virginia & Rainy Lake headquarters was moved from Sand Lake to Cusson, 30 miles north of Virginia, a new logging community named in honor of Samuel J. Cusson, general manager of the company, who had come to Minnesota from Cusson, Wisconsin where he managed Hines' logging operations. Upon his death in 1919 Cusson was succeeded

Edward Hines No. 22 at the head end of a log train near Cusson, Wisconsin. This former Pennsylvania Railroad H1 Consolidation worked earlier on the Washburn & Northwestern, a Hines road in nearby Douglas County. Finally she became V&RL No. 15 and hauled logs in northern Minnesota until 1929. She was scrapped in Duluth during 1935. — HOWARD PEDDLE COLLECTION

Baldwin-built Consolidation No. 14, the newest locomotive on the Virginia & Rainy Lake roster, arrived in 1913. — PEDERSON'S PHOTO STUDIO — FRANK KING COLLECTION

Duluth, Virginia & Rainy Lake construction train on newly laid track a few miles north of Virginia in 1902. Little No. 1, a 1902 Porter Mogul, is dwarfed by the four-wheel caboose ahead of it. — MINNESOTA HISTORICAL SOCIETY (BELOW) Frank Gillmor, V&RL general logging superintendent, rides in the back seat of a converted Model T rail car in this 1917 scene. — ST. LOUIS COUNTY HISTORICAL SOCIETY

as general manager by Thomas Whitten, who had previously managed lumbering operations for Hines at Winton and Hayward. Frank Gillmore, an able logger and railroader, was in charge of Virginia & Rainy Lake logging operations. He had come from Weyerhaeuser's Mesabe Southern, which he managed from 1902 through 1909. At Cusson, the Virginia & Rainy Lake Company erected new railroad machine shops, offices, rooming houses, a general store, school, theater, and recreation hall. The new town took pride in its water works and sewer system, refinements until then unheard of in a logging community.

Over the years Virginia & Rainy Lake constructed almost 150 logging camps and operated some 150 miles of main line, plus almost 1,500 miles of ever-changing branches or spurs — meandering around hills and spanning swamps, following the contours of the land into almost every corner of the North Country. Lakes from which logs were hoisted onto cars included Namakan, Kabetogama, Elbow, Black Duck, Johnson, Beaudoin, Ash, Elephant, and Echo.

During the 17-year period from 1912 to 1928 logging operations out of Cusson required a total of 1,422 miles of spur trackage, amounting to laying an average of 83.65 miles of railroad annually. To construct this much new track each year Virginia & Rainy Lake employed two 30-man steel gangs. Main branches were graded and ballasted; however, spurs leading into camps operating for a single winter, or made to extend over soft ground, were often constructed in temporary fashion by laying down stringers on the ground to support the cross ties. In extremely wet areas the stringers were laid on top of a corduroy of cross timbers.

With as many as 100 miles of spurs a year to build, the steel gangs seldom stopped working. One occasion when they did involved a somewhat humorous incident concerning a steel gang foreman known

A flat-bottom boat, known as an *alligator*, used in booming and towing logs across lakes by V&RL. — PETE BONESTEEL COLLECTION

126

Four Clyde-built Decker log loaders await disposition at Virginia one year after the closing of the V&RL mill in 1929. — PEDERSON'S PHOTO STUDIO — FRANK KING COLLECTION

The V&RL material offered for sale in 1930 included some 300 flat cars. Note stencelling on the car reading The VR&RL Co. — PEDERSON'S PHOTO STUDIO — FRANK KING COLLECTION

as "Single Eye" Frank, whose gang supposedly ceased operations for an entire afternoon in order to search for his glass eye. The story goes that the gang was lowering steel rails down a steep hill by tying a rope to the steel and then wrapping it around a tree, thereby easing the rail down slowly. During the process the bark broke loose, making it difficult to snub the rope. One by one, the men lost their grip on the rope, until only "Single Eye" Frank was left holding the end of it. Unable to snub the rope alone, he was whirled around the tree so rapidly that his glass eye popped out and flew into the brush.

In 1918 the Virginia & Rainy Lake Company owned 14 locomotives, 345 logging cars, four boxcars, one refrigerator car, one Bucyrus steam shovel, and a pile driver. In addition there were ten rail-mounted log loaders and a number of service cars on the roster. During the winter, when logging activities were at their peak, the company supplemented its motive power fleet with locomotives leased from nearby mining companies and regular main line railroads. One winter it leased over 20 locomotives, bringing its total in the woods to 37.

Each year saw logging operations extending farther away from the main line, resulting in increased demands upon the Duluth, Rainy Lake & Winnipeg (later the Duluth, Winnipeg & Pacific) for sufficient rail and fittings to construct necessary new trackage. This problem became especially acute during the 1920's, when there was an almost constant flow of correspondence between the company and the railroad on the subject. Although the latter was at times unable to fulfill requests for rail, it is doubtful that Virginia & Rainy Lake logging operations were ever seriously curtailed for lack of steel. When it could not obtain enough, the company met its needs by removing rail from lines temporarily out of use

and later relaying it, a practice that merely required more track laying than would otherwise have been necessary.

During its operations out of Cusson, Virginia & Rainy Lake employed a year-round average of about 1,700 men in the woods. In the key period from October 1 to April 1, however, some 3,000 to 4,000 men would be working in the forests. During the winter of 1921-22, at which time the average wage amounted to $1.68 per ten-hour day, eight camps were in operation.

The "long whistle" that blew at 4:19 P.M. on October 9, 1929 and signalled the passage of the last log through the big mill and the end of 20 years of continuous operation dealt a heavy blow to the community of Virginia. Loss of the Virginia & Rainy Lake Company and its giant facility for lack of raw materials was a local tragedy and caused an exodus of workers to Oregon, site of new Hines operations. Most of the Virginia & Rainy Lake Company's trackage was removed the next year.

Although it had been the largest and most impressive logging and lumbering enterprise of all time in Minnesota, as a business venture the Virginia & Rainy Lake operation north of Virginia proved disappointing to its investors. The high prices paid for the timber, the high logging costs necessary to remove it from remote and scattered timber tracts, and the heavy expense of the long rail haul to the mill at Virginia combined to render profits on finished lumber marginal. When it was all over, its owners could take comfort in little more than having recovered their initial investment.

To the west of the Virginia & Rainy Lake Company's operations, the International Lumber Company built and operated an extensive system of logging railroads, largely in Koochiching County. Con-

ceived by Minneapolis lumberman E.W. Backus, this company carried on all logging and railroading for the affiliated Minnesota & Ontario Paper Company (MANDO). International Lumber owned a large sawmill at International Falls and a local common carrier railroad, the Minnesota, Dakota & Western, which had been incorporated in 1902 as the International Bridge & Terminal Company.

The Minnesota, Dakota & Western served the International Lumber Company mill, as well as other industries at International Falls, and provided a connection with Backus' International Lumber Company logging railway complex to the south. Even as late as 1919, it was that lumberman's grandiose dream to extend the Minnesota, Dakota & Western some 200 miles west into the Dakota wheat fields, whose grain could then be hauled to huge flour mills to be constructed at International Falls. Minnesota, Dakota & Western plans did call for extending its line to Loman westward to the Minnesota Northwestern Electric Railway, thereby gaining entry into Thief River Falls, from where an extension could have reached into North Dakota. The flour mills were never built, however, and the Loman Line of the Minnesota, Dakota & Western reached only 18 miles west of the Falls and was abandoned in 1947.

In 1941 the Minnesota, Dakota & Western was operating 46 miles of line, including trackage rights

International Bridge & Terminal No. 7 was owned by the MD&W and carried as No. 7 on their roster. The little 0-6-0 was built by Baldwin in 1889 for the Joliet & Blue Island Railroad. — HAROLD VAN HORN

128

over the Northern Pacific between International Falls and Little Fork, where a connection was made with International Lumber's Deer River Line. At the time, the road owned six steam locomotives and 348 freight cars. It is presently controlled, through stock ownership, by the Boise Cascade Corporation and functions as a switching and terminal road.

Backus' International Lumber Company constructed and operated an estimated 1,000 miles of logging railroads over its 28-year lifespan from 1909 to 1937. During peak operations in 1917 the company operated 11 locomotives, some of which undoubtedly came from the Minnesota, Dakota & Western, and 150 logging flatcars, as well as a number of other items of rolling stock, including cabooses, steam shovels, work cars, and fire fighting cars. The greatest logging railway mileage was attained during 1928, when 150 miles of main line and 70 miles of spurs were in operation. Besides hundreds of millions of board feet of logs hauled to the sawmill at International Falls, the logging railroad carried, between 1914 and 1937, some 2 million cords of pulpwood, or an average of 5,000 carloads a year.

International's principal logging line extended from a point on the Minnesota & International south to Craigville on the Big Fork River. Its Deer River Line, constructed between 1912 and 1914, contained the longest stretch of tangent track on any logging railroad in Minnesota — a distance of 22 miles between mile post 10 and Camp 29. Logging headquarters and the enginehouse were at Camp 29, from where spurs extended down into northern Itasca

By the late 1940's, Minnesota, Dakota & Western No. 101 a Consolidation, her long logging career over, was relegated to switching duties at International Falls. — KOOCHICHING COUNTY HISTORICAL SOCIETY (BELOW) Three engines of the Minnesota, Dakota & Western bask in the summer sun on a Sunday afternoon during 1946 — FRANK KING

A Clyde track machine was photographed at work on the International Lumber Company's operation. Picking up and relaying as high as 100 miles of logging railroad in a single year, the company found that use of such machines saved time and money. — FRANK KING COLLECTION

MD&W No. 101 was built by Baldwin in 1913 for road service. Tender coal boards were applied during 1922 to enable this Consolidation to handle log trains on the Camp 35 turnaround within the 16 hour limit. — HAROLD VAN HORN

MD&W water car No. 2291 was used for fire fighting. — KOOCHICHING COUNTY HISTORICAL SOCIETY

International Lumber Company Heisler geared locomotive No. 2 in storage. — HAROLD VANHORN

130

A Minnesota & Ontario Paper Company
Clyde-built Decker loader transfers pulp-
wood from sleighs to rail cars. — KOOCHI-
CHING COUNTY HISTORICAL SOCIETY (BELOW)
A large slide jammer decking and loading
cars on the International Lumber Company
lines circa 1930. — MINNESOTA HISTORICAL
SOCIETY

A Minnesota & Ontario Paper Company (MANDO) Decker is shown loading a flat car. This scene shows how the empty flat moves through the machine during the loading process. — KOOCHICHING COUNTY HISTORICAL SOCIETY

An International Lumber Company section crew with their *Armstrong Tampers* near Camp 29. — KOOCHI-CHING COUNTY HISTORICAL SOCIETY

County and east into northern St. Louis County. Log hoists for loading cars were located at Loman on the Minnesota Dakota & Western; at Craig on the Deer River Line; at Beaver Brook on the Galvin Branch; on the Cutfoot Sioux at Round Lake; and at Harrigan Lake on a spur off the Nett Lake extension of the Holmstrom spur. Backus also planned to join his International Lumber Company's Deer River Line with the Minneapolis & Rainy River, which ended on the south bank of the Big Fork River at Craig; but though the two lines halted on opposite banks of the river, the necessary connecting bridge was never constructed.

Signs of the demise of the International Lumber Company's rail operations which by then were taken over by the Minnesota & Ontario Paper Company (MANDO) appeared on the horizon around 1938. By 1941 all the timber it needed was being moved by truck. To move up to 3,000 cords per day, during peak operations between the woods and the mills, 300 trucks were required. The advent of World War II only temporarily interrupted the transportation transition. Shortages of gasoline, tires, etc., gave the logging railroad a renewed lease on life, and during the conflict all forest products were handled by rail whenever possible. With the cessation of hostilities, however, MANDO operations reverted to trucks, which were capable of direct woods-to-mill delivery without a reload. While most of the big saw logs were gone, pulpwood for paper production — thanks to modern conservation and forest management practices — was still in abundant supply. The end of rail operations came during the summer of 1947 with removal of 32 miles of steel between Craigville and Little Fork. The scrapping was conducted by the James Construction Company of St. Paul.

International Lumber Company main line at Camp 29 shows the water tank and warehouse buildings. — KOOCHICHING COUNTY HISTORICAL SOCIETY

This General Electric-built gas-electric rail motor car No. 101 once figured in Minnesota, Dakota & Western's plan to extend their line westward to the Dakota wheat fields. The car carried the name of Minnesota Northwestern Electric Railway on its letterboard. — HAROLD VAN HORN

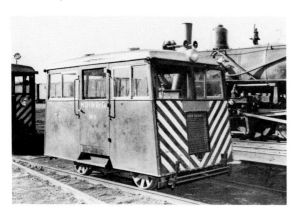

MD&W rail bus No. 9 was used to transport loggers between civilization and International's logging Camps. — KOOCHICHING COUNTY HISTORICAL SOCIETY (RIGHT) MD&W gas motor car was converted by the Oneida Manufacturing Company from an open combine in 1923. She is shown here heading a mixed train at Loman.

Still another company with a logging railroad in this northwestern area of Minnesota was General Logging of Cloquet, which had a substantial stand of timber on the Nett Lake Indian Reservation. During 1928 this firm constructed a 35-mile railroad from Gheen (on the Duluth, Winnipeg & Pacific) to the reservation. Originally, General Logging had planned to acquire the Virginia & Rainy Lake railroad shop and headquarters facilities at Cusson and extend its railroad from that point. Finding the terrain west of Cusson too rough, however, it rejected that site in favor of Gheen.

7

RED RIVER LOGGING

Large stands of pine of excellent quality were found in that portion of Minnesota, extending west of Leech Lake and south of Red Lake toward the Red River, which formed parts of Beltrami, Becker, and Cass counties. T.B. Walker of Minneapolis, possessed of sufficient capital to buy heavily in the 1875 Duluth Land Sale, became an important early timberland holder in Beltrami County. By 1883 he had acquired enough timber in the Clearwater area to warrant building a sawmill at Crookston in the Red River Valley.

Walker chose Crookston as the site for his mill because it lay below the confluence of the Red Lake and Clearwater rivers and Jim Hill's St. Paul, Minneapolis & Manitoba Railway passed through there on its way north to the Canadian border at St. Vincent. The Red River Valley, with its rich black soil, was being promoted for settlement by the road. The St. Paul, Minneapolis & Manitoba had inherited an extensive land grant along this portion of its line, formerly belonging to the old St. Paul & Pacific, which assured a steady market in the valley, as well as in future settlements to the west, for Walker's lumber.

Early logging operations in this section involved extensive use of streams and rivers for driving logs to the mills. Walker's were carried on by Sumner Bagley, a former Maine logger, who during the mid-1880's had constructed an elaborate system of dams and reservoirs on the Clearwater River. All logging took place in the winter and required sleighs and horses. To this day traces of the old sleigh roads, many of which were as well-graded as some logging railroads, can be seen in the area.

Walker's Red River Lumber Company cut 45 million board feet of lumber at Crookston during 1889, all of it coming from Beltrami County. He now began to buy timberland in the West, and to formulate plans for disposing of a portion of his huge Minnesota holdings in order to finance such acquisitions. The Panic of 1893 placed him in a distressed financial situation and, in company with Minneapolis lumbermen Akeley and the Pillsburys, he disposed of 1.5 billion board feet of pine north of Brainerd to the Minnesota Logging Company, a giant new concern formed by other prominent Minneapolis lumbermen. In 1897 he sold his Crookston mill and the timber tributary to it to the Shevlin-Carpenter interests, but retained considerable timber near Bemidji.

The following year Walker built a mill and a new townsite named Akeley, after his associate in the venture. The nearby community of Walker on the

135

Many of the early day photographs taken in the woods were captured by employees without regard to technical quality of a perfectly composed scene. This view of No. 1 of the Nichols-Chisholm Lumber Company at work amongst the white pines is a perfect example. At this late date a picture of No. 1 even if through the trees is better than nothing at all. — MINNESOTA HISTORICAL SOCIETY

Lumberman Thomas B. Walker was once the largest holder of timberlands in Minnesota. — MINNESOTA HISTORICAL SOCIETY

Planing mill of the Red River Lumber Company as it appeared on an old postal card. — J. M. MOSHER COLLECTION

shores of Leech Lake had hoped the new mill would be located there. Too many saloons in the town honoring his own name was given as the reason for Walker's choice of another site, for Akeley flatly prohibited such establishments. A more logical reason, however, was Akeley's position on the Great Northern Railway's Park Rapids line then under construction. When logs were later moved from the Solway area west of Bemidji, it was possible to handle them over a single railway, the Great Northern, all the way to Akeley. (Citizens of Bemidji had also wanted Walker to build a mill in their community. They complained that all the logs were either being loaded out or passing through.) At any rate, by 1912 Akeley boasted a population of 2,700, most of whom earned their livelihoods in the sawmill or in the woods. The sawmill, planning mill, and box factory alone furnished employment for 800 men the year around.

In 1901 the Red River Lumber Company constructed a logging railroad off the Great Northern at Wheelock, a small station about three miles west of Solway. The line extended approximately 15 miles south to Mallard Lake, where the townsite of Mallard was platted. In addition to a general store, Mallard had two hotels, a restaurant, the usual saloons, and a bank. Logs from the surrounding area were sleigh hauled to Mallard Lake for hoisting and loading onto cars. Today, except for a few shallow excavations in a field, nothing remains to mark the location of the town. In 1907, to reach additional timber, the rail line was extended approximately seven miles to Squaw Lake.

Red River Lumber Company crews and engines handled log trains over their line to the connection with the Great Northern, which railroad supplied all cars used in the operation. Trains were then handled by the Great Northern via Cass Lake and moved south to Akeley over the Park Rapids line — a total distance of 73 miles. The Red River Lumber Company ultimately operated an extensive network of logging railroad spurs, reaching as far as 25 miles from the Great Northern main line and connection with that railroad near Akeley. Although the lumber company owned four locomotives, including one

Red River Lumber Company used "Big Wheels" for summer skidding in Minnesota. Various types of two-wheeled log haulers were used in the Minnesota woods to bring logs from woods to landing or to the mill. Diameters of the wheels ranged from 8 to 12 feet. In woods words "Big Wheel" was the main camp boss. — MINNESOTA HISTORICAL SOCIETY

Great Northern Mogul No. 469 was leased by the Red River Lumber Company for use on their logging lines near Akeley. — BEMIDJI STATE UNIVERSITY HISTORY DEPT.

137

Camp No. 4 of the Red River Lumber Company was located on McCarty Lake spur. — BEMIDJI STATE UNIVERSITY HISTORY DEPTARTMENT

One of the carriages at the Red River Lumber Company sawmill at Akeley which was acquired from the Brooks-Scanlon mill at Scanlon in 1910. — BEMIDJI STATE UNIVERSITY HISTORY DEPARTMENT

Shay, it leased large Mogul engines from the Great Northern for main line haul to the mill.

During 1909 the mill at Akeley, which had a capacity of 350,000 board feet per day, was destroyed in a spectacular fire. A new mill was immediately erected on the same site. Included in the restoration was a hot pond in Eleventh Crow Wing Lake, heated by steam supplied from the mill's large refuse burner. Logs from the woods could then be received year-round for daily thawing out and cutting. The company advertised the new facility as "the most consistent producing mill in the country," and the mill made much of its willingness and ability to saw special items "to order" in 24 hours from tree to car.

In 1915 the Red River Lumber Company ceased operations in Minnesota and moved to Westwood, California, where Walker had some years earlier purchased 870,000 acres of prime timber. During 1917 the remainder of its logging lines were torn up and the rails shipped to France for the Military Railway Service.

A few miles southwest of the Red River Lumber Company's Mallard Lake operation, the Nichol-Chisholm Lumber Company operated an inland logging railroad in Clearwater and Becker counties. In 1904 this company, a Shevlin partnership, gained control of the Commonwealth Lumber Company, whose mill was located at Frazee on the main line of the Northern Pacific Railroad. Shortly after 1906 Nichols-Chisholm acquired some 150 million board feet of pine from the Indians on the White Earth Reservation, paying $8.50 per 1,000 board feet.

Construction of Nichols-Chisholm's railroad started in 1908, by which time it had proven impractical to sleigh haul timber to the landing on Commonwealth Lake. Logs were hauled to various points along the company's line, loaded onto cars, and railed to Commonwealth Landing at Elbow Lake. There they would be dumped from the trestle at the landing, assembled into booms, towed across a chain of lakes, and driven down the Otter Tail River to the mill at Frazee. After the annual freeze-up, logs would be stockpiled on Elbow Lake throughout the winter, and an unusual method was devised to move loaded log cars out on the ice for dumping. A heavy sleigh with short rails attached by spikes to its bunks would be backed up to an elevated spur track near the landing, and a loaded log car would be shoved out onto it. The car was securely blocked, then hauled out on the ice by a team of horses and its logs dumped from the sleigh. By this means cars could be dumped at random locations on the lake, thus avoiding excessively high piles of logs.

Headquarters for the Nichols-Chisholm logging operation was located on Long Lake south of Bagley, and consisted of an office, enginehouse,

A Nichols-Chisholm wood-burning Shay locomotive spots Russel cars for loading by a slide jammer which moves itself along the tops of the cars while loading. It was unusual to load logs from a trestle as shown in this scene. — MINNESOTA HISTORICAL SOCIETY

blacksmith's shop, two bunkhouses, and a store. All supplies had to be freighted in. During peak logging activity the company employed a total of 500 men at headquarters and in its camps.

Motive power on the road consisted of an ancient American-type rod engine and three Lima Shays. The rod engine, the first to arrive, was appropriately referred to as *The One Spot*. The first Shay arrived new in 1907 and became engine No. 2. The other two Shays, which came later, were No. 3 and No. 4. All of these locomotives were wood burners. According to local lore the first three engines were moved on their own wheels to the closest point on the Red River Lumber Company's Mallard Line, where they were dismantled and hauled overland through the timber to Nichols-Chisholm headquarters by large Case steam tractors.

Locomotive No. 1 was usually assigned to haul log trains between Headquarters Camp and Commonwealth Landing at Elbow Lake. The slower but more powerful Shays handled all hauling on the rough spurs which reached into the timber.

Estimates are that 25 to 40 miles of railroad were usually in operation at a given time. Standard train length on the Nichols-Chisholm main line was 26 cars, and all locomotives and cars were equipped with air brakes and link and pin couplers.

The Nichols-Chisholm railroad was abandoned and its tracks removed during 1917, and the sawmill, which had a capacity of 250,000 board feet per day, ceased operation a year later. Old engine No. 1 was cut up for scrap in the woods, and the three Shays were dismantled and moved overland to Park Rapids, where they were reassembled and shipped out by rail to new owners.

To the south and east of Lower Red Lake were sizable stands of superior pine, much of which stood on the Red Lake Indian Reservation. By treaty the Indians ceded a large portion of the reservation in return for annuities, goods, and improvements, thus opening these timberlands to private timber cruisers who quickly located and estimated the better stands. Prior to opening the land for sale, the United States government sent in its own agents to estimate the value of the timber.

Public sales of former reservation timbered land took place in Crookston and Duluth during July 1896, with some 115,000 acres (estimated to contain 226 million feet of pine) being offered. Among participating lumbermen were the Shevlin-Carpenter Company of Minneapolis, the Weyerhaeusers, and Wright and Davis. The bidding lumbermen had all made their own surveys and were much more fully aware than the government's representatives of the actual amount of timber involved. Shortly thereafter the possibility of fraud was raised and further sales were stopped until the lands had been re-surveyed by cruisers selected by the Department of the Interior. Only after passage of the Morris Act in 1902, which required sale of timber by bank scale, did timber sales begin bringing in a fair amount of return to the Indians and the federal government. Although lumbermen disapproved of the Act, it gave them one advantage in that it required them to pay only for the stumpage (standing timber) and not the land itself.

Logging on reservation timberland acquired before the Morris Act had begun in 1895, when the Arpin Brothers of Wisconsin constructed a camp at Nebish to log and land logs on Mud River. Unusually deep snows that winter halted this operation, and the following year the Arpins' contract with the Crookston Lumber Company (owned by Shevlin-Carpenter of Minneapolis) was awarded to the Halvorson-Richards Company, a firm that had only recently completed work on the Chicago Drainage Canal.

Mud River proved unsatisfactory for driving logs, and eight miles was too far to sleigh haul; consequently, plans were revised to include a logging

Nichols-Chisholm Shay No. 4 ended her days working for the Connors Lumber & Land Company in Wisconsin where she was photographed in 1933. — JAMES P. KAYSEN

Lumber storage yards of the Nichols-Chisholm Company at Frazee as photographed in 1910. — DAVID RITCHIE COLLECTION

railroad from Nebish to Red Lake. The St. Hilaire Lumber Company of Minneapolis sought permission from the Department of the Interior to construct such a line, which was granted on June 25, 1897. Under its terms, which would probably satisfy even today's most ardent environmentalists, the company was to be allowed to:

Construct a temporary railroad for the purpose of transporting timber to market from a point about two miles East of the township line of township 153 range 33, on the South boundary line of the retained Red Lake Indian Reservation Northward, a distance of about 8 miles to the shore of Red Lake, following as nearly as practicable the bank of Mud River, on the following conditions:

(1) That the said Railroad will be only used for the purpose of transporting the saw logs of said lumber company from their logging camps to said lake, and supplies from the lake to their camps and *not* for the general purposes of a Railroad; and that it shall be for *temporary* and not permanent purposes.
(2) That the said St. Hilaire Lumber Co. will remove said road as soon as it has answered these purposes, and at their expense.
(3) That the said company bind themselves not to cut any ties on said ceded reservation or commit any waste or damage on same except what is necessary in the construction of said road-bed.
(4) That this privilege may be revoked at any time by the Secretary of the Interior.
(5) That they recompense the Indians for any damage said road may cause the Indians, said damages to be determined in such manner as the Secretary of the Interior of the Indian Commission may direct.
(6) That said company will give Bonds in such sum as the Secretary of the Interior may direct for the performance of said conditons.

Since the Great Northern had not yet built through Bemidji, rails and other equipment had to be freighted overland from distant railheads. From the end of the Brainerd & Northern Minnesota Railway at Walker light rails, a boiler, and other parts for a small locomotive were transferred to barges, towed to Steamboat Landing on the north shore of Steamboat Lake, and stored for winter sleighing to Nebish. Trucks for the logging cars were transported by boat from Thief River Falls up the river and across Red Lake to Red Lake Landing. From there they were hauled over the partially completed grade to Nebish, where the cars were assembled. The first engine to arrive at Nebish was reputedly a small Baldwin Vauclain compound 0-4-4 Forney-type steam locomotive, which had recently been retired from service on

Red Lake Transportation Company locomotive No. 1 was identical to Wisconsin, Ruby & Southern Railway No. 1 shown in this photograph. Both engines were Baldwin Vauclain Compound Forneys received from the Chicago South Side Elevated Railway. — JAMES P. KAYSEN — LARRY EASTON COLLECTION

Chicago's South Side Elevated upon electrification of that line.

Halvorson-Richards immediately went about enlarging the camp facilities left by the Arpin Brothers on Nebish Lake, and also built an office and car shop there. A wye was located at Nebish to change the direction of locomotives, and a trestle and hoist were constructed on the lake for loading logs onto cars for movement to Red Lake.

On December 9, 1897 the Red Lake Transportation Company was chartered, with a capital stock of $100,000, to commence business on January 1, 1898 and run for a period of 30 years. The general nature of its business was to be:

the construction, maintenance and operation of railroads, owning and operating steam and towboats for transportation of passengers, freight and logs, also buying, owning selling and dealing in lands and tenements and merchandise of all kinds.

This company acquired the St. Hilaire Lumber Company's partially finished line, and in 1899 completed the road from Red Lake Landing to Nebish.

By March 1900 the Red Lake Transportation Company had banked some 25 million board feet of pine at Red Lake Landing. During the previous four months one of its small logging contractors, Mulroy Brothers, with a crew of only nine men and four

horses, cut and skidded to the railway over an average distance of one-half mile more than 1-½ million feet of logs. The *Mississippi Valley Lumberman*, commenting on their accomplishment, stated "such hustlers are not the kind of men who spend their time kicking on weather."

At Red Lake Landing (later renamed Redby) logs were dumped from the high bank, formed into booms, then towed to the outlet by steamboats and driven downstream to mills at St. Hilaire and Crookston. The Crookston Lumber Company had acquired the Crookston mill, along with Walker pine in the area, during 1894, when Walker sold a substantial part of his holding as a result of the financial panic, and it also operated the St. Hilaire mill.

Red Lake teemed with log booms and steamboats during the first years of this century. The steamers *Mudhen, Martin Lally, Jim Meehan,* and *Jim Anderson* were well-known in the earlier days. The *Beltrami, Chippewa, Margarite,* and *J.P. Kinney* arrived on the scene later. Years afterwards their rotting hulls could be seen reposing on the beaches near Redby. Each towboat was equipped with a "growser," a heavy piece of timber which could be dropped through an opening in the bottom of the boat to act as an anchor while the "spool" wound up the cable attached to a log boom.

During 1900 the Red Lake Transportation Company's road was extended 2.5 miles to Whitefish, and on February 12, 1903 the company acquired from the government title for a permanent right-of-way. At the time it owned two locomotives and 32 cars, including one caboose. The line, laid with 35-pound rail, still had no connection with the outside railroad world, and all equipment and supplies continued to be freighted in. In 1902 the car shop at Nebish burned to the ground, and this — along with other problems — forced the little company into receivership.

Red Lake Transportation Company's sternwheeler *Chippewa* and sidewheeler *Beltrami* saw service in the early years of this century pulling log booms and handling freight on the Lower and Upper Red Lake. — FRANK KING COLLECTION

Early photograph of Porter-built Mogul No. 3 of the Red Lake Transportation Company. She later became Minneapolis, Red Lake & Manitoba No. 3. — FRANK KING COLLECTION

142

Little Minneapolis, Red Lake & Manitoba No. 3 awaits orders at the Redby station before departing on her 33-mile run to Bemidji. Behind the string of empty log cars at the rear of the mixed train consist may be seen Lower Red Lake. — FRANK KING COLLECTION

The Minneapolis, Red Lake & Manitoba Railway Company was incorporated in Minnesota on June 15, 1904, and on June 28, 1904 it took over the property of the bankrupt Red Lake Transportation Company. The new company was capitalized at $100,000, and its officers included Minneapolis lumberman Charles A. Smith, president; Charles M. Amsden, secretary; Andreus Ueland, treasurer; and A.L. Molander, general manager. Grading from Nebish to Bemidji began in December 1904, and the road was opened for traffic on November 1, 1905. A proposed extension of the road to Minneapolis and to Winnipeg was also surveyed; but nothing ever materialized in this respect. The road had all it could do to make ends meet with only the 33.5 miles of line from Bemidji to Redby. The 2.5 miles of track from Nebish to Whitefish Lake were abandoned during 1905.

A view of the old MRL&M station at Redby as it appeared in 1953. Considering the age of the old station, it was in pretty good shape. — FRANK KING

143

A slight mishap resulted in MRL&M Mogul No. 3 lying on her side in the ditch. Coach No. 7 does not look the worse from the wreck. (BELOW) A "shoo-fly" was already constructed around the engine and a primitive crane appeared on the scene and ready to assist in getting old No. 3 back on the rails. — BOTH FRANK KING COLLECTION

Minneapolis, Red Lake & Manitoba water tank, engine house and repair shops at Redby. — FRANK KING COLLECTION

Because it was planning to build its own railroad into the area as an outlet for its timber, the Crookston Lumber Company opposed the Minneapolis, Red Lake & Manitoba extension to Bemidji. Fearing that the Red Lake road would afford other lumbermen an advantage when it came to bidding on reservation timber, Crookston Lumber even went so far as to circulate petitions among its employees and supporters urging them to object to platting of Redby as a townsite.

When its efforts to halt extension of the Minneapolis, Red Lake & Manitoba into Bemidji proved fruitless, Crookston Lumber rapidly pushed construction of its own line, the Wilton & Northern Railroad, from Wilton on the Great Northern to Island Lake, 24 miles north. The line paralleled the Minneapolis, Red Lake & Manitoba, coming within 1.5 miles of it in the vicinity of Campbell and Peterson Lakes. A branch was constructed to Boston Lake, where logs were hoisted onto cars. Another hoist was located on Island Lake, at the end of the road, only a mile south of the reservation line. The town of Island Lake, with a store, post office, and a few saloons, was a pleasant little community situated on the shore of the lake. Wilton & Northern headquarters and enginehouse were at Fowlds, about mid-way on the line.

A company store run by John Fowlds (for whom the town was named), post office, lumber company bunkhouse, boarding house, bank, a few hotels, and the usual saloons made up this community, of which nothing remains today other than faint outlines of former buildings and a few locomotive cinders.

Until 1912 the Wilton & Northern Railroad normally handled all timber logged by its parent Crookston Lumber Company. In 1908, however, rather than conveniently ship Whitefish Lake logs over the Minneapolis, Red Lake & Manitoba to its mill at Bemidji, Crookston Lumber stubbornly drove them to Red Lake and down the Red River to its mill at Crookston. Usually, however, logs were taken to Wilton for movement to Bemidji by the Great Northern. Eventually, largely due to the efforts of A.L. Molander, a reconciliation took place between the Minneapolis, Red Lake & Manitoba and Crookston Lumber. A connection was constructed between the Minneapolis, Red Lake & Manitoba spur at the Nebish gravel pits and Island Lake, after which

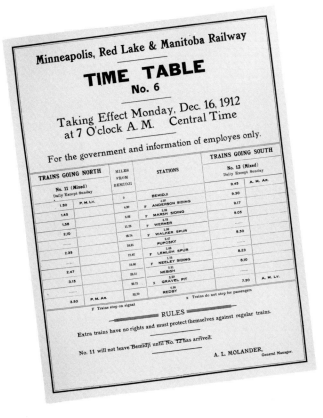

Employees time table of the MRL&M for December 16, 1912, showed a mixed train daily between Bemidji and Redby, a distance of 32 miles. The running time for this distance was approximately two hours and twenty minutes. — FRANK KING COLLECTION

A Crookston Lumber Company steam hauler with a long train of sleighs. A look through a sharp magnifying glass shows 15 loads, which was quite an undertaking for a steam hauler. — FRANK KING COLLECTION

Crookston logs moved to Bemidji over the Red Lake line instead of by way of Wilton. Strangely, this operation lasted only one summer. Wilton & Northern rails were removed in 1914, and the towns of Fowlds and Island Lake began to fade into oblivion.

Some years later the Crookston Lumber Company carried on extensive logging railroad operations out of Keliher on the Minnesota & International Railroad, at the end of the branch extending north from Funckley. In addition, from 1919 to 1922 they operated 30 miles of spurs off the Minnesota & International near mile post 123, and during that period maintained a spur off the same road near Gemmel. The company also put in a camp on Neeley Siding at mile post 19.60 on the Minneapolis, Red Lake & Manitoba to handle timber north of there, the last of which was cut at Mud Lake north of Puposky during 1925 and 1926.

Freight tonnage over the Red Lake Road reached record levels during World War I. Within the five year period from 1916 through 1920 the little road moved almost 1,000,000 tons of freight. This tonnage consisted mainly of white pine sawlogs most of which were cut on the Red Lake Indian Reservation by lumberman E.W. Backus. Some 100,000 acres of excellent white pine had been set aside in the newly formed Red Lake Indian Forest in 1916 and Backus was the successful bidder on 50,000 acres of it when put up for sale the following year. The cut was 105 million board feet for which the Red Lake Indian Fund in Washington collected $1,395,500 from the International Lumber Company.

The final big timber movement over the Minneapolis, Red Lake & Manitoba began in 1926, when the International Lumber Company (Backus and Brooks) bid successfully on the remaining Indian reservation pine lands. This timber moved over the newly constructed 11-mile International Lumber logging line to the Minneapolis, Red Lake & Manitoba north of Nebish at mile post 28, and over the

Lineup of Crookston Lumber Company motive power in front of the enginehouse at Keliher. The following locomotives can be seen as identified from left to right in the above scene. They are engine No. 2, an old Northern Pacific 4-4-0; the "One Spot," a Climax geared locomotive; and Lima Shay No. 10. — DAVID RITCHIE COLLECTION

latter road to Bemidji. International Lumber Company also constructed 22 miles of spurs on the reservation. Between Bemidji and International Lumber's mill at International Falls the logs traveled over the Minnesota & International Railroad.

International Lumber Company's cost breakdown for its Red Lake logging operation during the 1926-27 season reads as follows:

INTERNATIONAL LUMBER COMPANY
RED LAKE OPERATION — LUMBER SCALE
Season 1926-27

LOGS:				Quantity	Rate/M	Amount
Sawing				48,754,280 ft	1.16	$ 56437.57
Skidding & Hauling				48,754,280	2.44	119337.31
Camp Spurs				48,754,280	2.58	125819.49
Roads & Landings				48,754,280	.40	19424.23
Overhead				48,754,280	2.10	102531.84
				48,754,280		
Cost Landed					8.68	423550.44
Car Loading				49,732,270	.86	42527.33
Car Loading Labor	49,732,270	.44	21725.51			
Car Loading Service	49,732,270	.42	20801.82			
Train & R.R. Service				49,732,270	.52	25768.04
Gen. Admin. & Whse. Exp.				48,754,280	.35	16932.84
Cost at Spur 28				48,754,280	10.41	508778.65
Freight to Int'l Falls					3.67	179013.65
COST AT INT'L FALLS					14.08	/M687,792.32

NOTE: Transportation related expenses amounted to approximately 75 percent of the total cost of logs delivered to the mill at International Falls.   Track construction costs per mile for main line trackage averaged $3,400 and for spurs $2,300 for this operation.

Broadside of Crookston Lumber Company Shay No. 4 showing the vertical engine assembly which was the trademark of the Shay geared locomotive. — DAVID RITCHIE COLLECTION

Crookston Lumber Company Shay No. 4 near Funckley on the Minnesota & International. The white flags on front of the engine indicate a special movement over the M&I. — DAVID RITCHIE COLLECTION

A steam skiddler, also equipped with a special steel tower, at work near Keliher for the Crookston Lumber Company. Note that the skidder is resting on corner blocking permitting empty flat cars to pass through during the loading process. A locomotive was always on hand to spot cars during this loading procedure, but was not captured in the scene. This skidder machine and tower was moved on a flat car between loading sites. — DAVID RITCHIE COLLECTION

Crookston Lumber Company No. 1 was one of only three Climax geared locomotives used in Minnesota. The Climax was an ususual locomotive. Its cylinders were parallel to the frame of the engine, but sloped at an angle of 45 degrees. The drive was through a propellor shaft to geared axles. It was slow but high-powered and filled a need on temporary and rough track. — DAVID RITCHIE COLLECTION

Minneapolis, Red Lake & Manitoba No. 4 about to depart Bemidji for Redby with the "mixed." This Ten-Wheeler was built by Baldwin in 1912. The author is owner of one of her builders plates. — HAROLD VAN HORN COLLECTION

Minneapolis, Red Lake & Manitoba wooden combination car No. 10 was acquired from the Missabe Road. The baggage section was added to the car after it came from the original owner. — HAROLD VAN HORN

The closing of the Crookston Lumber Company mill at Bemidji in 1926 foreshadowed the demise of the Red Lake road. Declining pulpwood shipments and a few carloads a week of refrigerated fish from Redby were not enough to keep the line which was never very profitable at best, operating in the black. Economy moves instituted by the Molanders included replacement of the Ten-Wheeler which normally handled the mixed train with a gas motor car capable of towing an occasional express refrigerator of fish. The end came with completion of an all-weather hard-surface highway between Bemidji and Redby during the early 1930's. Trailer rigs then skimmed off what little traffic was left, and in 1937 the Minneapolis, Red Lake & Manitoba applied to the Interstate Commerce Commission for permission to abandon, not granted until May 1938.

Rails were picked up in 1939, and the right-of-way, including the company telephone line, was sold. That same year the road's last locomotive, engine No. 4, a trim Baldwin capped-stacked Ten-Wheeler, was sent to Duluth for scrapping. With the passing of the Minneapolis, Red Lake & Manitoba, the Duluth & Northeastern gained the distinction of being the only remaining common carrier logging railroad in the state.

The Crookston Lumber Company mill at Bemidji cut up its last log in 1926. — FRANK KING COLLECTION

Railroad camp on the Twomey-Williams logging railroad. This type camp was one in which all the buildings were made to fit on railroad cars. This included bunk cars, kitchen cars, and cars for camp and logging supplies. Such railroad camps were not commonly used in Minnesota. (LEFT) Train of long pilings moves over the logging railroad belonging to the White Cedar Timber Company near Big Fork. — BOTH FRANK KING COLLECTION

The last non-common carrier logging railroad in the area was operated by Twomey-Williams' White Cedar Timber Company. This 33-mile line, which functioned between 1923 and 1937, connected with the Minnesota & International at Big Falls. Its motive power consisted of two steam locomotives and one 20-ton Plymouth gasoline locomotive. Standard flatcars for log loading were supplied by the Minnesota & International. Saw logs were shipped via the Minnesota & International and the Great Northern to the Cloquet Lumber Company at Cloquet until the closing of the mill in 1927. After that date Twomey-Williams cutting consisted largely of piling, poles and pulpwood.

The White Cedar Timber Company's 33-mile long railroad was the last logging railroad in the Big Falls region. Consolidation No. 1 with her crew near Big Falls sometime during the 1920's. The company owned two rod engines and the gasoline engine shown above. — TUFFORD COLLECTION

8

LOADING THE CARS

Loading logs onto cars was a major operation on the logging railroad. Given the ever rising costs of production and transportation, improved log loading methods and equipment were always topics of prime interest to lumbermen.

Steam-powered log loaders or "jammers" were available as early as the 1880's; but they were crude and seldom used. The most popular means of log loading in Minnesota was the time-tested "cross haul" method, which had been used for years in loading sleighs. In the cross haul, two skids (logs) were laid extended from the ground to the car and then a chain or cable, referred to as a "loading line," was wrapped around the log to be loaded and moved over the log car by a team of horses, thereby hoisting the log in place on the car.

A loading crew was comprised of four men on the ground, plus the top loader on the car and a teamster to handle the horses. Loading called for a good deal of skill and speed, and these crew members were among the best paid workers in the woods. A good top loader was always in demand and considered "king of the camp."

Around 1900 the steam loader, or jammer — as it was popularly referred to in the woods — took over on most rail loading operations. By then side stakes were generally used on the cars, eliminating "corner binds" with wrapper chains. The skill required of the top loader diminished with the introduction of the steam loader, whose operator assumed much of the former's distinction. A tripod was usually erected, with a steam "donkey" engine furnishing power for lifting the logs onto cars at locations where logs were hoisted from lakes. Steam-driven endless conveyor-type chain hoists were also used at such sites by the Virginia & Rainy Lake Company and by Swallow & Hopkins.

A prerequisite for steam loaders was that they be self-propelled, either on the rails or along the tops of the cars. The Clyde Iron Works of Duluth developed and produced two basically similar types of self-propelled on-track log loaders. There was also the slide loader, which pulled itself by means of a cable along the tops of the cars as they were loaded. The Barnhart was another type of loader which moved itself along the tops of the cars. In this case the log cars were equipped with a rail along each side, upon which the small flanged wheels of the loader supported and guided the machine. To this writer's knowledge the Barnhart loader was never used in

153

Loading cars near Duluth around 1890 by means of the cross-haul method. This method took a lot of brute strength. The man on top was known as the "Top Loader." (LEFT) An early scene showing the use of an "A" frame and horse power for the loading of cars. Note the unusual bark marks on the log in the foreground. — BOTH MINNESOTA HISTORICAL SOCIETY

Double tripods were used for loading logs on the Brainerd & Northern Minnesota. Note the wood rack car in the foreground used for supplying fuel to the two boilers. — FRANK KING COLLECTION (LEFT) Loading poles at a Page Hill camp using a gin pole with a swinging boom. A single horse on the cross haul furnished the power to hoist the poles. — MINNESOTA HISTORICAL SOCIETY

Slide jammer loading cars with piling near Big Falls. — FRANK KING COLLECTION

Loading logs from a lake by means of a steam hoist with an endless chain on the Virginia & Rainy Lake company. — PETE BONESTEEL COLLECTION (BELOW) Alger-Smith Company's Decker No. 5 loading Russel log cars along the Duluth & Northern Minnesota Railway in Lake County. — FRANK KING COLLECTION

Minnesota logging operations. The American Hoist & Derrick company of St. Paul, Minnesota, however, constructed a similar log loading machine.

Periodically, new steam-powered log loaders of various kinds were developed and tried out. In 1895 the *Mississippi Valley Lumberman* reported on the Kaime log loader, which was to be tested on the Brainerd & Northern Minnesota Railway. Its loading mechanism consisted of adjustable skids, located on the end of a flatcar, with the boiler and hoisting equipment at the other end. The skids were provided with endless chains, upon which dogs retained the logs while being carried up to the car being loaded. The loader was self-propelled by means of a gear and chain connection to one of the trucks. It was mentioned that one of these machines was used by the Lyman Lumber Company of Necedah, Wisconsin, which found "they had such a good thing that they decided to give the rest of the world a chance." The Brainerd & Northern Minnesota was likewise impressed with the Kaime loader and purchased three of them. One major drawback to the Kaime machine was that it required spotting on a track directly adjacent to the cars being loaded. This problem was subsequently overcome, however, by the two types of loader produced by Clyde.

In 1901 the Red Lake Transportation Company announced testing of a steam-operated slide jammer developed by its own G.A. Westman, which it claimed was "one of the best and fastest log loaders in the northwest, barring none." It further asserted that the hoister would load 200,000 board feet of timber a day in any kind of weather. In view of the performance of other loaders, the stated capability of Westman's machine would appear to have been overly optimistic.

Details and drawings showing the Decker Self-Propelling Log Loader taken from a Clyde Iron Works catalog of parts. The drawing shown below shows how the rails over the trucks permit the passage of log flats for loading. — **FRANK KING COLLECTION**

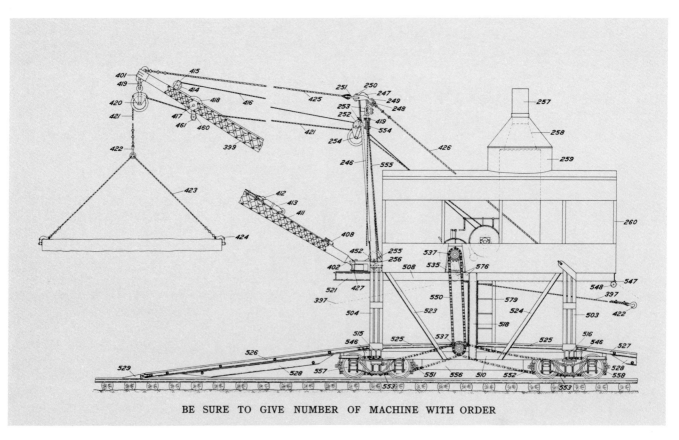

BE SURE TO GIVE NUMBER OF MACHINE WITH ORDER

The McGiffert Loader was probably the last of the big old-time railroad machines. The loader was first used in the South, and was most popular in the West. It probably was the best known of all the loader types. The side view shown above is from the Clyde Iron Works Catalog. — FRANK KING COLLECTION

In northeastern Minnesota and northern Wisconsin, the Clyde-built Decker and McGiffert loaders were popular, while in the western part of Minnesota the slide jammer was preferred. The Crookston Lumber Company became one of the greatest proponents of the latter.

These Decker and McGiffert loaders were such interesting examples of specialized logging railroad equipment that a brief description of their construction and operation seems in order. The Decker loader remained on its own trucks at all times when loading and while moving along the track. An open space for the passage of empty log cars was provided above the trucks and under the machinery deck. Steel rails, laid through the machine on the lower deck, con-

nected with an inclined track reaching down to the main rails on each end of the machine. The empty train of log cars was shoved through to the rear of the machine, usually by means of a locomotive, and each car was then pulled forward in front for loading by a drum-powered cable on the machine. The Decker was available in various sizes and track gauges, ranging from three feet to standard.

The McGiffert loader, developed by John R. McGiffert, a Duluth attorney with a flair for mechanics, differed from the Decker in that the empty cars passed through on the main line without the machine's being jacked up on supports. It carried the loading mechanism on a platform supported above the track by means of four curved standards or

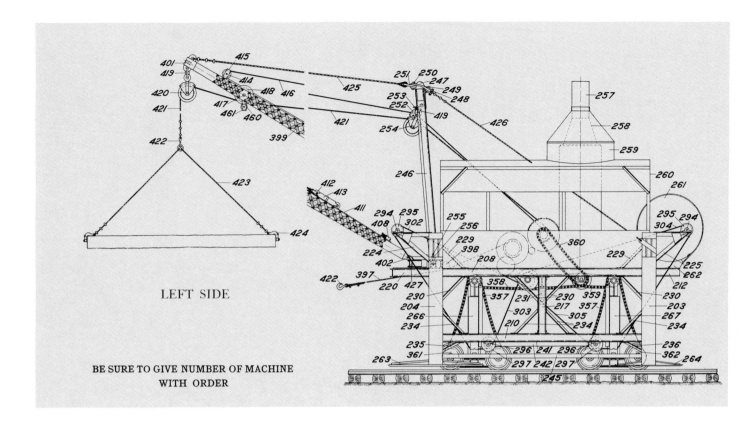

LEFT SIDE

BE SURE TO GIVE NUMBER OF MACHINE
WITH ORDER

Detailed drawings of parts of the McGiffert Loader taken from the Clyde Iron Works Catalog. Note the cover illustration which shows how the trucks were drawn up under the carbody permitting log cars to pass through during loading. — FRANK KING COLLECTION

158

legs, terminating in long shoes which rested upon the ends of the ties outside the rails when the machine was in operation. For passage of empty cars, the trucks were drawn up under the machinery deck. This allowed the loader to settle down on the ends of the ties, leaving the track beneath clear for cars to pass between the supporting standards. With a crew of four or five men, the McGiffert loader could easily load between 120,000 and 130,000 board feet of logs per day. A single machine of this type, under most favorable conditions, has been known to load in excess of 500,000 board feet per day.

Both the Decker and the McGiffert loaders were self-propelled and capable of moving empty log cars as they moved between loading sites. For this reason they did not require the standby services of a locomotive to spot empty cars for loading. The slide jammer could also load cars on the same track upon which it stood and move itself and a few of them along for short distances by attaching its cable to a tie or a tree stump. To move between loading sites involving any appreciable distance, however, it required a locomotive.

The McGiffert was also popular on the Pacific Coast, where larger models were employed. The largest loaders of this type were equipped with six- or eight-wheel trucks, instead of the four- or two-wheel ones used in the Lake States. The McGiffert machine used in the heavy timber of the West was usually equipped to do skidding, in addition to loading, with 500 to 600 feet of skidding distances being practical. Drums for holding 100 to 1,500 feet of cable were supplied when desired. The McGiffert loader was so well-accepted within the logging industry that John McGiffert left his law practice to devote full time to running the Clyde Iron Works, which became a leader in manufacturing log loading equipment. Today the company no longer makes such machines, specializing instead in the design and construction of huge whirley cranes capable of lifting as much as 2,000 tons!

Rail-mounted steam-operated log skidders, which were popular in the Pacific Northwest during the heyday of railroad logging, found little favor with loggers in Minnesota. The Crookston Lumber Company, the only concern in the state which used the steam skidder with any degree of success, employed such equipment in the Blackduck, Kelliher, Mizpah, and Northome areas from 1910 to 1920. A number of other companies, including Alger-Smith and Cloquet Lumber, experimented with high-line cable skidding with little success. It can be concluded that Minnesota's easier terrain was much more conducive to animal-powered skidding than the mountainous topography found in the western states.

Skidding costs were closely watched by the logging camp foreman. Whenever possible he made

Today, only three McGiffert Loaders are known to exist. Two are located at the Collier Logging Museum in Oregon and one in Duluth which was donated to the Lake Superior Museum of Transportation by the International Paper Company. — BLAMEY'S STUDIO (BELOW) A horse jammer loading logs on a Duluth & Iron Range spur. — FRANK KING COLLECTION

A McGiffert Loader with a rigid boom, the trucks raised and cars passing through. — FRANK KING COLLECTION

Another view of a McGiffert Loader with the trucks raised showing the clear space for the passing through of cars during the loading operation. — FRANK KING COLLECTION

The "Whistle Punk" was a man or boy who passed signals from the rigging slinger to the donkey engineer when yarding logs or to the engineer of a loader. This was often the starting job on a logging crew. (LEFT) A large rail-mounted skidder with a steel tower owned by the Crookston Lumber Company. — BOTH J. C. RYAN COLLECTION

160

A high-line steam skidder at work loading Russel cars on the narrow-gauge Crescent Springs Railroad in Wisconsin during the 1890's. Note the spar tree looming above the cab of the locomotive. — HOWARD PEDDLE COLLECTION

every effort to confine skidding length to a distance not exceeding one-quarter of a mile from the nearest sleigh haul road or railroad spur. Most skidding was conducted in early winter, before the snow became too deep. A single team of horses and one man could skid up to 150 logs in a single day.

While efficient for its time, such log loading equipment as has been described in this chapter seems crude by present standards. Today's logging, largely conducted by truck, has introduced sophisticated log cutting, gathering, and loading equipment with capabilities far beyond the wildest dreams of early Minnesota loggers.

McGiffert Loaders built for western logging operations were ponderous machines. They were used for skidding and loading, had cables for haul back, etc. — FRANK KING COLLECTION

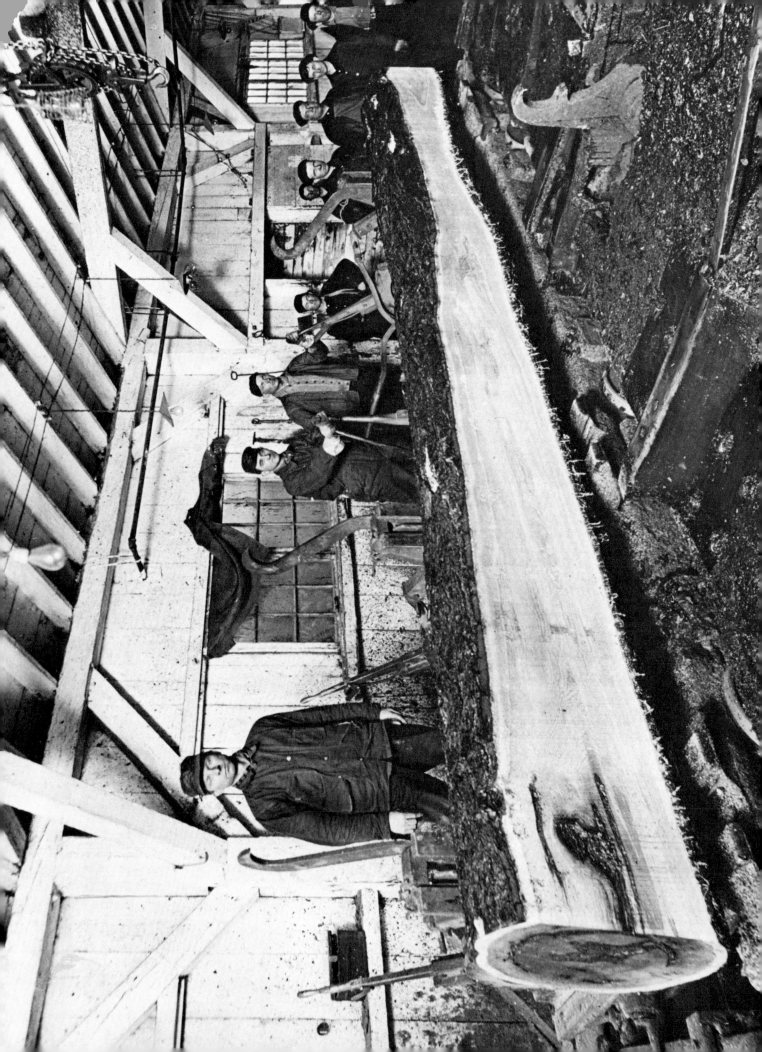

9

THE GREAT SAWMILLS

Sawmills were usually located on a navigable river or lake to take advantage of low-cost water transportation for log movement. In 19th-century Minnesota the large sawmills concentrated in Minneapolis at the Falls of St. Anthony made use of the Mississippi not only for delivery of logs from pine lands tributary to the river, but for water power with which to operate. In like manner the thriving little lumbering community of Cloquet on the St. Louis River 20 miles west of Duluth initially received the bulk of its log supply by water and derived power for an early mill from Knife Falls. Duluth mills, strategically situated at the head of Lake Superior, found the lake a useful transportation artery for rafting logs from operations on both shores. Duluth mill operators also availed themselves of the economies of water transportation down the Great Lakes for lumber destined for eastern or foreign markets.

While Minneapolis, Duluth, and Cloquet were considered great sawmilling centers, many other Minnesota communities were also notable in that regard. Significant among the earlier mill locations were Stillwater and Winona. Virginia became the site of the giant Virginia & Rainy Lake mill, the world's largest white pine plant. Important mills functioned at Akeley, Baudette, Bemidji, Brainerd, Cass Lake, Crookston, Deer River, Frazee, International Falls, Little Falls, Nickerson, Scanlon, Spooner, Thief River Falls, Tower, and Winton.

In terms of annual output the Minneapolis mills represented the greatest collective capacity of any sawmilling complex in Minnesota. Total lumber production peaked at 594 million board feet during 1899, a figure more than double that attained a decade earlier. Among the larger Minneapolis producers that year, with annual output expressed in millions of board feet, were C.A. Smith Lumber Company, 108.3; H.C. Akeley Lumber Company, 108; Backus-Brooks, 96; Nelson-Tenny Lumber Company, 70; Diamond Mill, 45.5 Shevlin-Carpenter Company, 38.7; Carpenter-Lamb Company, 37,5; and Bovey-De Laittre Lumber Company, 34.3. Naturally, the bulk of the logs for Minneapolis mills arrived via the Mississippi River, although after 1900 rail transportation was employed to overcome mill shortages caused by log jams or periods of low water.

By the turn of the century the great river-based Minneapolis mills were on the decline; but the lumber output of Duluth, on Lake Superior, was still

163

The Knox Lumber Company mill at Winton on Fall Lake. — PAUL SILLI-MAN COLLECTION

The Mitchell & McClure mill in Duluth was one of the largest in the country when built in 1891. This mill was sold to Alger-Smith in 1902. — ST. LOUIS COUNTY HISTORICAL SOCIETY

Panoramic view showing some of the many sawmills which were operating along the St. Louis Bay waterfront in West Duluth during the 1910 period. The mills are easily identified by the sawdust burners. Note the log booms in the bay at the center right. — FRANK KING COLLECTION

164

The Garfield Avenue Mill of Alger-Smith was located on Rice's Point at the foot of the
Interstate Bridge in Duluth. Alger-Smith also operated the former Mitchell & McClure mill
in West Duluth. — ST. LOUIS COUNTY HISTORICAL SOCIETY

One of the earliest sawmills in Duluth was the one operated by the Scott-Graff Company. It was also the last mill to operate in Duluth, closing in 1925. — ST. LOUIS COUNTY HISTORICAL SOCIETY

In the early days of the 20th century, it was not uncommon to have as much as 500 million board feet of lumber waiting shipment on Duluth's waterfront. In this scene, the Missabe Road's fire tug *McGonagle* pumps water at the rate of 12,000 gallons per minute on the LeSeuer Mill fire which destroyed 18 million feet of lumber valued at $500,000 on July 10, 1909. — FRANK KING COLLECTION

growing. In 1902 Duluth reached a peak output of over 440 million board feet. This figure exceeded the entire annual white pine lumber output of the state of Michigan, once the world's greatest producer.

Duluth mills were booming, and the industry represented the largest employer in the city at the time; however, their future was becoming a matter of considerable speculation among lumbermen. During August 1902 the *Mississippi Valley Lumberman* reported pessimistically that five of the 13 mills at the Head of the Lakes would soon be without local standing pine, and reminded its readers that the necessity for mill operators to go farther into the interior for their log supplies would mean higher costs. Around 1910 Duluth's six large sawmills were nevertheless cutting nearly 1.5 million board feet of lumber per day and employing almost 2,000 men in the process. Mill work plants were also busy making cabinets, sashes, doors, furniture, and other articles produced from wood.

Alger-Smith's two mills at Duluth produced an average cut of 600,000 board feet of lumber per day, which became the greatest daily production of any lumber company in the city. These two facilities employed a total of 600 men, and the company was the city's largest employer at the time. The Virginia & Rainy Lake mill at Duluth averaged 250,000 board feet of lumber per day and employed some 300 men. Other firms which operated large mills in the city included Scott-Graff, Mullery McDonald, and Red Cliff — whose daily outputs were 200,000; 250,000; and 140,000 board feet of lumber respectively.

Duluth's mills were all located along the waterfront in the western part of the city, and estimates

This vessel called a "Lumber Hooker" belonged to the Edward Hines Lumber Company. It was one of scores which once plied between Duluth and lower lake ports in the lumber trade. — FRANK KING COLLECTION

Finished lumber is being transferred from rail cars to lake vessels at the Northern Pacific lumber dock in Duluth about 1910. — FRANK KING COLLECTION

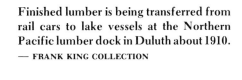

The steamer *Hilton,* her decks stacked high with what appears to be pulpwood, heads for an unknown destination. — FRANK KING COLLECTION

were that during the winter close to .5 billion board feet of lumber were stored in mill yards and docks awaiting shipment. Few cities in the nation were as favorably situated as Duluth for the shipment of lumber. With docks on one side and rails on the other, it could be transported to all parts of the country at low cost and with great dispatch. During 1915, however, lumber production at Duluth fell below 100 million board feet. Ten years later it would end forever with the closing of the Scott-Graff mill.

The following is an attempt concisely to describe the working processes of a typical Minnesota sawmill. Logs arriving by rail were run out on a dump trestle laterally inclined to promote rapid unloading from log cars and located along one side of the mill pond or extending into the pond. The logs were dumped and stored in the mill pond to await delivery to the plant. Inasmuch as logging railroads made possible year-round deliveries, "hot ponds" created by utilizing surplus exhaust steam from the mill were universally employed to keep the ponds from freezing over in the winter.

Mill pond of the International Lumber Company at International Falls, showing men with pike poles guiding logs to the endless chain which carried the logs up the jack slip into the mill and the awaiting saws.
— MINNESOTA HISTORICAL SOCIETY

Interior of the International Lumber Company's mill showing the giant double band saw squaring off a log being advanced by the carriage. Upon passing through the band saw, the log is rotated 90 degrees and the carriage reversed, removing another slice from the log. After being squared off, the timber is advanced through a gang of saws and cut into finished lumber. — MINNESOTA HISTORICAL SOCIETY

The choice of logs for a day's cutting was made by the pond tender upon instructions from the mill superintendent. Since sawmills often cut for special orders or by contract, log ownership was determined by the stamp mark driven into the ends of each. Pikemen used long poles to select the proper logs and direct them to the jack slip, an endless chain device equipped with spikes which seized and carried them up an incline into the mill. Mid-way in their ascent a ring of high-pressure water jets washed the logs free of all sand, gravel, or other foreign material that could prove injurious to the saws.

The jack slip deposited the logs onto an inclined log deck to await their turn on the carriage. Most of the larger mills were equipped with double head-saws. Logs entered between them and were directed to either side onto the log deck feeding a particular saw by means of a mechanical kicker.

The first operation in the mill involved squaring off the logs by running them back and forth through a single-band head saw while they were supported on the carriage. Four or five trips on the carriage were usually enough to square off each side of a log. This process was carried out at an extremely fast pace with the sawyer controlling the movement of the carriage and re-positioning of the log. (In the pine country a "sawyer" is called a "faller," and in some places a "bucker" is called a "sawyer.") Because of the high noise level in the area the sawyer communicated with his co-workers in intricate sign language. He was a key man, and his skill determined to a great extent the quality of the lumber and the profitability of the operation.

The squared timbers, or cants — as the men called them — were then sent to the gangsaw, which quickly sliced them into boards of the desired thickness. Because of their thin kerf (thickness of cut), bandsaws — which cut down on waste — were usually preferred to circular saws. The exception occurred in mills specializing in heavy timbers. Since reduction of waste was not a major concern in their operation, these were more often equipped with circular saws.

The side cuts, those boards produced from squaring up a log, were sent through an edger which trimmed away bark from both edges. The edgings were carried away and cut into short lengths which were usually converted into lath. From the bandmill, the boards moved to an inspection table where they were graded, trimmed to specified lengths, and then sorted for drying and curing.

Finished lumber moved from the mill to the drying and storage area on small flatcars over a narrow-gauge tramway system. Some of the larger mills employed small steam locomotives or battery-operated motors for moving long strings of such cars. The green boards were sorted by grade and size and

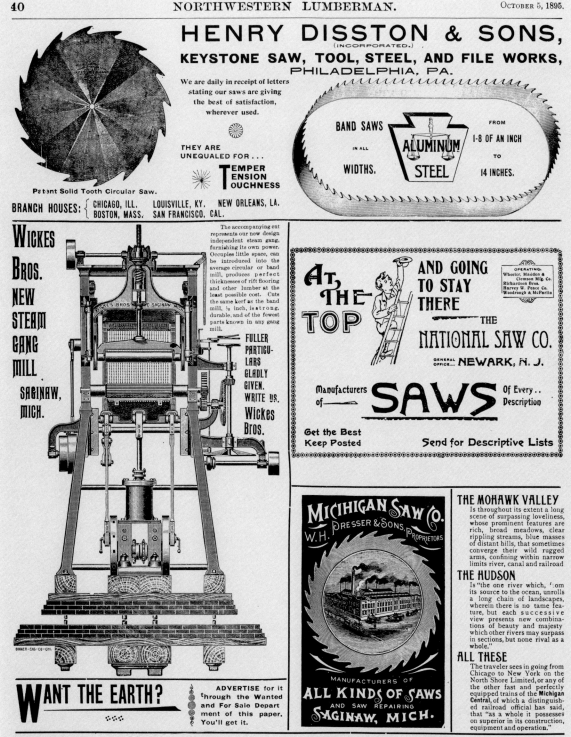

Advertisement from the October 5, 1895 issue of the *Northwestern Lumberman*, showing various types of saws used in the lumber mills. — HOWARD PEDDLE COLLECTION

Birdseye view of the Red River Lumber Company lumber storage yard and mill at Akeley, Minnesota. — PETE BONESTEEL COLLECTION

Workmen stacking lumber for curing from one of the flatcars belonging to the mill tramway system. — DONALD DUKE COLLECTION

Two "Hay-Burners" switch box cars at the Knox Lumber Company mill in Winton. — MINNESOTA HISTORICAL SOCIETY

stacked to great heights for six to twelve months of curing. Within the first month, a white pine board was expected to shed 50 percent of its weight. As a result of this evaporation of moisture in wood cells, the atmosphere of a sawmill community was permeated with a delightful, pungent, refreshing odor that was much stronger than the aroma of the pine forest from which the timber had been cut.

Upon completion of drying and as directed by sales the cured lumber was either moved to the planing mill for dressing to finished dimensions or shipped out rough to be finished by the buyer at some distant location. The bulk of the billions of board feet of lumber shipped through Duluth to eastern markets was in rough form.

Just as they varied in size, sawmills varied in their equipment. Given an identical set of mill requirements, few lumbermen would agree on the best types and make of equipment to be used. At times mill design appeared more a matter of personal opinion than lumber science. The little pioneer Paine Company mill at Carlton, for example, which contained only a single rotary saw, specialized in cutting large timbers for railroad and bridge use. Mitchell & McClure's big mill at Duluth, constructed during 1891, was equipped with one rotary, one band, one Rossier, and two 42-inch Wickes gangsaws. This facility was capable of turning out 250,000 board feet of lumber per ten-hour shift. Nearby, a similar sized mill operated by Merrill & Ring covered 53 acres of land on Duluth's waterfront and boasted about its 800 steam-horsepower capacity and its perfect lighting by means of electricity. A narrow-gauge Porter 0-4-0 tank locomotive was kept busy moving cars of green lumber between this mill and its storage yard for drying and curing.

At the time of its construction in 1901 Brooks-Scanlon's mill at Scanlon was one of the largest and most complete plants in the United States. The main

Two views of the Brooks-Scanlon mill at Scanlon circa 1902. At the time of its completion this was one of the most modern sawmills in the country. — MRS. L. RIEL COLLECTION

mill building, 84 x 250 feet in size and one of six in the complex, housed a single-gang three-band plant, whose capacity without crowding was 350,000 board feet in a ten-hour shift. Most of the machinery was furnished by the Diamond Iron Works of Minneapolis, which guaranteed that with its equipment a mill would cut ten percent more lumber in a given time than any other comparable mill on the market. The steam engines powering the Brooks-Scanlon mill were to that date the biggest ever made for the purpose and were constructed by the Twin City Iron Works, which also supplied the largest refuse burner then in existence — a giant 35 feet in diameter and 100 feet in height. This mill operated for only eight years before being dismantled and shipped to Florida, and few signs of it remain at its original site. Piling which once supported log cars as they dumped their contents into the mill pond is visible north of the St. Louis River highway bridge, and along the south side of the highway the circular brick foundation of the great burner stands sentinel near the river bank. A historical marker, however, identifies the spot.

Three miles up river from Scanlon, the sawmilling center of Cloquet took pride in its identity as the "home of the white pine." Located there were five Weyerhaeuser mills, two each operated by the Cloquet Lumber Company and the Northern Lumber Company, and one by the Johnson-Wentworth Company. With the exception of one water-powered facility, they were steam-operated. From 1902 until 1917 total annual lumber output at Cloquet consistently ran around 250 million board feet. In 1919 the two Northern Lumber Company mills ceased operating,

The Skibo Timber Company mill, located at the end of the Duluth & Iron Range Skibo mill spur, was of modest size by Minnesota sawmill standards. — FRANK KING COLLECTION

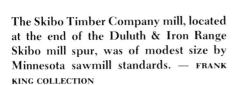

The Johnson-Wentworth sawmill was one of five owned by Weyerhaeuser at Cloquet. — E. A. KRUGER COLLECTION

The origins of Clouquet Lumber Company's water-powered mill on the St. Louis River at Cloquet date back to 1883. — E. A. KRUGER COLLECTION

however, and during 1927 both the Cloquet Lumber Company and Johnson-Wentworth closed their mills, thus bringing an end to nearly 50 years of highly profitable sawmilling. Fortunately for Cloquet, its future — unlike that of most other sawmilling centers — was not completely dependent upon lumber production. Due largely to the foresight of the Weyerhaeusers and others, forest products have continued to supply the life's blood of the community. Today the Northwest Paper Company, Conwed Corporation, and Diamond Match turn out an array of products using wood from northern Minnesota's forests that would have been unimaginable in the era of the colorful lumberjack.

The largest sawmill in Minnesota was operated by the Virginia & Rainy Lake Company at Virginia, on the Mesabi Iron Range, 70 miles north of Duluth. Employing two ten-hour shifts, this giant mill complex, formed in 1909, could produce 1 million board feet of lumber per day. It consisted of two large sawmills, a planing mill, dry-sheds, and lumber piling yards, occupying in all over 300 acres. Daily when working a two-shift operation the mill shipped out 50 carloads of lumber, plus several carloads of lath. It employed over 1,300 men and claimed to be the world's largest pine manufacturing plant. Another 3,000 to 4,000 men were employed by the Virginia & Rainy Lake Company in the woods and on its logging railroad.

To distribute the green lumber from the mill to piles for curing, there were more than 17 miles of tramways and 60 miles of track over which it was moved by steam locomotives and battery-operated electric motors. Upon drying and per sales demand

View showing the immense Virginia & Rainy Lake lumber storage yard at Virginia. (UPPER LEFT) Electric motors handled the lumber from sorting chain to the storage yard. (LEFT) View of the Virginia & Rainy Lake loading track at the planing mill and warehouse where 27 cars could be accommodated under cover at one time. — ALL PETE BONESTEEL COLLECTION

Electricity to power the Mesaba Railway interurban cars was generated from slabwood and sawdust in their power station located at the nearby Virginia & Rainy Lake sawmill. This scene was photographed during the winter of 1913 with interurban No. 17 and a trailer car running down the main street of Virginia. — WAYNE C. OLSEN COLLECTION

173

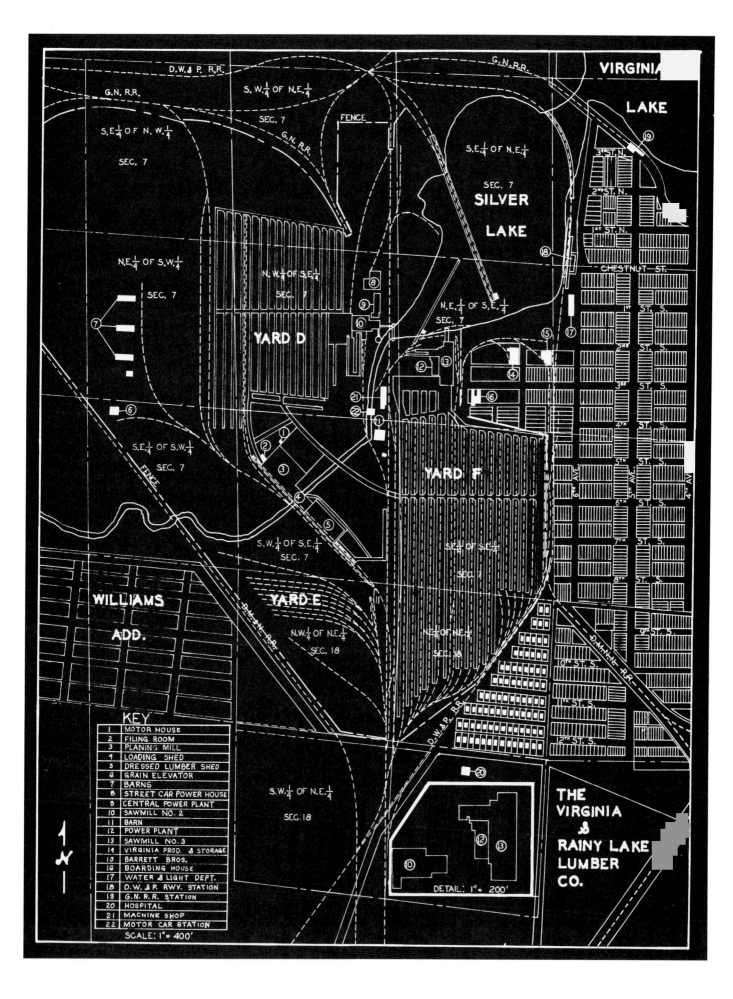

THE
VIRGINIA
&
RAINY LAKE
LUMBER
CO.

KEY

1	MOTOR HOUSE
2	FILING ROOM
3	PLANING MILL
4	LOADING SHED
5	DRESSED LUMBER SHED
6	GRAIN ELEVATOR
7	BARNS
8	STREET CAR POWER HOUSE
9	CENTRAL POWER PLANT
10	SAWMILL NO. 2
11	BARN
12	POWER PLANT
13	SAWMILL NO. 3
14	VIRGINIA PROD. & STORAGE
15	BARRETT BROS.
16	BOARDING HOUSE
17	WATER & LIGHT DEPT.
18	D.W.&P. RWY. STATION
19	G.N.R.R. STATION
20	HOSPITAL
21	MACHINE SHOP
22	MOTOR CAR STATION

SCALE: 1" = 400'

DETAIL: 1" = 200'

WILLIAMS ADD.

YARD D

YARD E

YARD F

SILVER LAKE

VIRGINIA LAKE

The sawmill of the International Lumber Company at International Falls, the last of the big mills to operate in Minnesota. This mill cut up its last log in 1937. — MINNESOTA HISTORICAL SOCIETY. (OPPOSITE PAGE) A map showing the Virginia & Rainy Lake Lumber Company's giant sawmill complex at Virginia, Minnesota. — DUANE KRENZ COLLECTION

boards were transferred to the huge electrically-driven planing mill for dressing. An adjacent dry-shed boasted a capacity of over 3 million board feet of dressed lumber, and there a wide assortment of grades, sizes, and patterns was always on hand to expedite the filling of orders.

In the year 1937 the era of big-time sawmilling in Minnesota came to an end, when the International Lumber Company's big mill at International Falls cut up its last log. The state which for many years met its own lumber needs and supplied the demands for lumber of much of the Midwest as well must now import lumber, most of it from the West Coast. Although several small portable-type mills are presently operating in Minnesota, their output is the merest trickle in comparison to that of the immense sawmills that once represented one of her most important industries.

Mikados Nos. 13 and 14, which arrived from the Baldwin Locomotive Works in 1913, were the last steam locomotives acquired by the Duluth & Northern Minnesota Railway. Upon cessation of logging operations in 1919, these Walschaert valve geared locomotives were sold to the ore carrying Lake Superior & Ishpeming. No. 14 has been preserved and will find a permanent home at the Lake Superior Museum of Transportation at Duluth. D&NM Nos. 13 and 14 were the largest locomotives built for any Minnesota logging railroad. — FRANK KING COLLECTION

10
IRON HORSES IN THE WOODS

During Minnesota's logging era over 250 steam locomotives were in operation on the state's logging railroads. This figure includes motive power leased only during peak winter logging months from common carrier railroads and mining companies in the area.

With the average Minnesota rail log haul in excess of 50 miles from forest to mill, it was only natural that the rod-powered engine would be preferred, and over 200 locomotives of this type were employed. The conventional locomotives ranged across a spectrum from pre-Civil War 4-4-0's to powerful Mikados weighing 200 tons with tender. The Mogul was by far the most popular engine operating in the woods. She was fast, flexible, and easy on the track. The largest locomotives built specifically for a Minnesota logging railroad were the Duluth & Northern Minnesota's two 1913-built Baldwin Mikados, No. 13 and No. 14, each of which weighed 300,000 pounds with tender. The biggest locomotives ever to operate on a Minnesota logging railroad were General Logging's two ex-Cambria & Indiana Railroad Mikados, No. 90 and No. 91, each weighing 400,000 pounds with tender.

Numerous factors had to be taken into consideration in determining the proper size and type of locomotive demanded for a given service: trailing tonnage, ruling grades, degree of curvature, bridge-loading ratings, and — last but not least — weight of rail. Since most logging railroads were constructed as cheaply as possible, keeping rail weight to a minimum became a common means of holding down costs.

It may be asssumed that the maximum load light steel rails will carry, with crossties properly spaced, is 300 pounds on a wheel for each pound weight of rail per yard for rails weighing from 40 to 60 pounds per yard. In line with this assumption let us select the proper rod-type locomotive for two hypothetical logging railroads, one laid with 45-pound rail, the other with 60-pound rail. In either case the desired tractive effort of the locomotive is placed at 27,000 pounds, based on 25 percent adhesion and 108,000 pounds on the driving wheels.

The maximum weight per wheel for a locomotive operating on 45-pound rail is 13,500 pounds, or 27,000 pounds per driving axle. Four driving axles, therefore, are required to carry 108,000 pounds on

the drivers, which at 25 percent adhesion will produce 27,000 pounds tractive effort. In this case the locomotive required would be of the Consolidation or the 2-8-0 type.

Following the same calculations we find that the maximum weight per wheel for a locomotive operating on 60-pound rail is 18,000 pounds, or 36,000 pounds per axle. In this case only three driving axles are required to carry 108,000 pounds on the drivers. The Mogul (2-6-0) would be the proper selection.

Various types of geared locomotives built to run on meandering trackage found their way into the forests. An estimated total of 41 geared locomotives were used in Minnesota's woods. Included in this total were 34 Lima Shays, five Heislers, and three Climax locomotives. The Virginia & Rainy Lake Company and Swallow & Hopkins were the biggest users of Shays each having had five of them on its roster. General Logging used two of the five Heislers on its lines north of Lake Superior, and International Lumber Company operated one Heisler on its logging railroad complex near the Canadian border. Split Rock Lumber Company owned two of the Climax locomotives.

The geared locomotive excelled where grades were steep, being able to operate on inclines of 10 to 12 percent (trackage climbing 10 to 12 feet for every 100 feet). Geared power was equally at home on light rail and sharp curvature. Their main drawback, however, was speed. For this reason they were usually confined to spur tracks into timber where the haul was relatively short.

For the most part, the locomotive rosters of Minnesota's logging railroads consisted of second-

Mitchell & McClure Mogul No. 2 was built by the Brooks Locomotive Works in 1892. She was sold to the Duluth & Northern Minnesota in 1902, becoming their No. 7. The Mogul type was the most popular engine used in the woods. — FRANK KING COLLECTION

Lake Superior Piling Company three-truck Shay No. 4 became Virginia & Rainy Lake No. 22. She was built in 1898 for T.A. Blackwell, a Pennsylvania lumber firm. Shays often had several owners before terminating their long careers. — FRANK KING COLLECTION

Not all Shay geared locomotives in Minnesota were used in the woods. This 37-ton two-truck model was built by the Lima Locomotive Works in 1905 for the Consumer's Ore Company. — P. E. PERCY COLLECTION (BELOW) Duluth & Northeastern Mogul No. 21 had a long and useful career. She was built by Baldwin in 1907 to 5-foot gauge for the U.S. Government to haul dirt trains in the construction of the Panama Canal. She was re-gauged and later hauled logs in northern Minnesota by the time this photograph was taken in the 1950's. She had acquired a Northern Pacific headlight and a tender from a Western Maryland 0-6-0. — FRANK KING

hand and surplus motive power acquired from common carrier railroads or logging companies in other states. Exceptions to this were the fleets of locomotives owned by the Brainerd & Northern Minnesota Railway and the Duluth, Mississippi River & Northern Railroad. The Brainerd & Northern Minnesota's roster was unique in that it was comprised of 12 Moguls all of which had been constructed for that road. The Duluth. Mississippi River & Northern's motive power fleet was made up of ten engines all acquired new.

When a logging firm ceased operations geared motive power was the most negotiable type of locomotive. The bulk of these engines found new homes in other parts of the country upon completion of their Minnesota service. The majority of the rod locomotives lived out their useful lives in the state and were scrapped when logging operations ended. Exceptions were the Duluth & Northern Minnesota's two Baldwin-built Mikados. They were only six years old in 1919, when the road stopped hauling logs, and were sold to the ore-carrying Lake Superior & Ishpeming on the opposite shore of Lake Superior. Fortunately, one of these fine engines, Duluth & Northern Minnesota No. 14, has been spared the scrapper's torch and will eventually find a home at the Lake Superior Museum of Transportation in Duluth.

Cambria & Indiana Mikado's Nos. 7 and 8 became Nos. 90 and 91 on General Logging. These were the largest locomotives used on a Minnesota logging railroad. — GEORGE SENNHAUSER COLLECTION

180

APPENDIX

LIST OF MINNESOTA LOGGING RAILROADS

Lumber Company	Railroad Operating Name	Location	Miles of Main	Branches	Operating Years	Locomotives	Logging Cars	Remarks
Alger-Smith Lumber Co.	Duluth & Northern Minnesota	Knife River	100	350	1898-1921	14/R 1/G	500	Abandoned in 1921. North end used by General Logging Co.
Brainerd Lumber Co.	Brainerd & Northern Minnesota	Brainerd	82	50	1894-1900	12/R	500	Acquired by Minnesota & International in 1900. Now BN.
Brooks-Scanlon Lumber Co.	Minnesota & North Wisconsin	Nickerson	11	2	1895-1903	2/R	35	Company relocated at Scanlon in 1901. (Scanlon-Gipson).
Cloquet Lumber Co.	Duluth & Northeastern	Scanlon	55	11	1901-1912	10/R 1/G	265	Railroad abandoned in 1912.
		Rush Lake	27.5	10	1898-1904	2/R 1/G	78	Constructed by Duluth Logging & Contracting Co.
Crookston Lumber Co.		Cloquet	57	100	1904-	27/R 3/G 5/D	300	Present mileage 11.4 miles owned by Potlatch
	Wilton & Northern	Wilton			1905-1912	1/R 3/G		Operated off Great Northern at Wilton.
		Milepost 123	30		1919-1920	1/R 3/G		Operated off Minnesota & International milepost 123.
		Gemmel	5		1923-1924	1/R 3/G		Operated off Minnesota & International at Gemmel
		Kelliher	25			2/R 3/G		Operated off Minnesota & International at Kelliher.
Cross Lake Logging Co.	Northern Mississippi	Cross Lake	28	10	1890-1908	3/R	76	Railway acquired from St. Anthony Lumber Co. Isolated operation.
	Duluth & Iron Range	Various	35	40			600	Duluth & Iron Range hauled logs.
	Duluth, Missabe & Northern	Various		10			200	Duluth, Missabe & Northern hauled logs.
Dunka River Lumber Co.	Dunka River	Off D&IR	20		1915-1920			Duluth & Iron Range cars and locomotives used.
		Off D&IR Eastern Mesaba Branch	21		1910-1913			Operated off Duluth & Iron Range Eastern Mesaba Branch
Empire Lumber Co.	St. Croix & Duluth	Yellowbanks	21		1893-1899	3/R	50	Operation moved to Dedham, Wisconsin with same name used. Isolated operation.
Estate of Thomas Nestor	Estate of Thomas Nestor	Gooseberry River	25		1900-1909	3/R	87	Isolated railroad operation.
General Logging Co.	General Logging Co.	Cascade Jct.	114	70	1927-1938	4/R 4/G		Operated off Duluth & Northeastern.
		Winton	26		1923-1937	2/R		Operated off Duluth & Iron Range.
		St. Louis Jct.	20		1923-1928			Operated off Duluth & Northeastern.
Itasca Lumber Co.	Itasca	Gheen	35		1928-1939	1/R 1/G	60	Operated off Duluth, Winnipeg & Pacific
		Cohasset	10		1892-1897	2/R	60	Railroad moved to Deer River in 1897.
	Itasca (Became M&RR)	Deer River	-		1897-1904	4/R		Purchased by Minneapolis & Rainy River in 1904.
	Minneapolis & Rainy River	Deer River	98	15	1904-1932	12/R	382	Railroad abandoned in 1932.
International Lumber Co.	Minnesota, Dakota & Western	International Falls	46		1902-	12/R 2/G 5/D	350	Presently operated as terminal railroad at International Falls.
Kileen and Gillis	Killen & Gillis	Craig Line	123	1000	1909-1947	9/R 2/G	150	Locomotive leased from D&IR. Cars leased from D&NE.
		Red Lake Res.	11	12	1926-1930	1/R 1/G		
McAlpine, John	McAlpine Spur	Ellsmere	10		1920-1923	1/R		Operated over 4 miles of former Mitchell & McClure lines of Duluth & Iron Range.
		Milepost 39	8		1905-1907			Operated off DM&N near Saginaw. See Split Rock Lumber Co.
Merrill & Ring Co.		Nr. Saginaw	5		1898-1900			
Minnesota Land & Construction Co.	Duluth, Virginia & Rainy Lake	Virginia	90		1901-1911	5/R 5/G	200	Now part of Duluth, Winnipeg & Pacific (Virginia to Britt)
Mitchell & McClure	Mitchell & McClure Logging RR	Barker (NP)	25		1890-1899	3R 2/G	150	Had operating right over Northern Pacific to Pokegama Landing.
		Adolph	12		1899-1901	2/R		Operated off DM&N. Line sold to Minnesota & North Wisconsin.
		Milepost 39	13		1901-1902	2/R	83	Operated off D&IR. Line and equipment sold to Duluth & Northern Minnesota in 1902.
Mullery-McDonald Lumber Co.	Mullery-McDonald Lumber Co.	Iverson (NP)	10		1908-1915			Operated for Northern Lumber Co.
Nelson, C. N., Lumber Co.	C. N. Nelson Lumber Co.	Gowan	11		1890-1895	1/R 1/G	40	Operated off Duluth & Winnipeg.
Northern Lumber Co.	Mesabe Southern	Kinross (DM&N)	40		1895-1913	4/R 2/G	177	Built by C. N. Nelson. Sold to Northern Lumber in 1895.
		Hull Junction (DM&N)	15		1923-1924	2/R		
Nichols-Chisholm Co.	Nichols-Chisholm Co.	Park Rapids	30		1908-1917	1/R 3/G	60	Isolated railroad operation.

LIST OF MINNESOTA LOGGING RAILROADS (continued)

Lumber Company	Railroad Operating Name	Location	Miles of Main	Branches	Operating Years	Locomotives	Logging Cars	Remarks
Northern Mill Co.	Gull Lake & Northern	Lake Hubert	20	10	1890-1894	1/R	2/G 40	3-Foot Gauge. 12 miles sold to Brainerd & Northern Minnesota in 1894. (**) Minnesota's only narrow-gauge logging railroad.
North Star Timber Co.	North Star Timber Co.	Whyte (D&IR)	15		1917-1930	1/R		Used D&IR locomotives and cars on D&IR trackage.
O'Neal Brothers	O'Neal Brothers	Knife Lake	27		1895-1902	2/R	40	Logged for Laird-Norton Co. Rails sold to Nebagamon Lumber Co. in 1902. (**)
Paine, J. M., & Co.	J. M. Paine & Co.	Carlton (NP)	10		1886-1900	2/R	1/G 25	Minnesota's first logging railroad.
Pine Tree Manufacturing Co.	Pine Tree Manufacturing Co.	Remer (SOO)	20	30	1910-1916	1/R	3/G	Logs moved by Soo Line and Northern Pacific to mill at Little Falls.
Powers & Simpson Co.	Duluth, Missabe & Western	Barclay Junction	22	12	1898-1910	3/R	82	Logs moved by Great Northern in their cars to mill at Akeley.
Red River Lumber Co.	Red River Lumber Co.	Shevlin (GN)	27		1904-1915	2/R	2/G	
		Akeley (GN)	39		1904-1915	2/R	2/G	
St. Hilaire Lumber Co.	Red Lake Transportation Co.	Redby	12		1897-1904	2/R	32	Assets acquired by Minneapolis, Red Lake & Manitoba in 1904. (**)
(Became)	Minneapolis, Red Lake & Manitoba	Bemidji	34		1904-1938	5/R	60	Abandoned in 1938.
Sauntry & Cain Co.	Sauntry & Cain Co.	Akinson	7		1901-	1/R		Operated off the Northern Pacific at Akinson.
Scott & Holsten Lumber Co.	Scott & Holsten Lumber Co.	Drummond	10		1900-1905			Serviced by D&IR on D&IR's own trackage.
Scott-Graff Lumber Co.	Scott-Graff Lumber Co.	Ridge	11		1911-1917			Serviced by D&IR on D&IR's own trackage.
		Allen Junction	6		1915-1920			Serviced by D&IR on D&IR's own trackage.
Shank, N. B., Co.	N. B. Shank Co.	Summit (D&IR)	18		1909-1915	2/R		Line sold to Jack Saari in 1915. Taken up in 1925.
		Milepost 68.5	10		1909-1915	2/R		Operated off D&IR at Milepost 68.5.
Split Rock Lumber Co.	Split Rock & Northern	Split Rock River	2		1899-1906	1/R	2/G 62	Owned by Merrill & Ring Co. of Duluth. (**)
Swallow & Hopkins Lumber Co.	Swallow & Hopkins Lumber Co.	Winton (D&IR)	10	10	1899-1920	1/R	1/G 40	Portage Railroad sold in 1911 to St. Croix Lumber & Mfg. Co. (**)
		Winton	20		1909-1920	1/R	4/G	Line sold to Northern Lumber Co. in 1923.
Standard Lumber Co.	Leech Lake & Northern	Cuba Siding	17		1904-1908			Connected with Great Northern at Cuba Siding.
Swan River Logging Co. (Wright & Davis)	Duluth, Mississippi River & Northern	Swan River	50	60	1892-1899	10/R	200	Sold to James J. Hill in 1899. Became part of Great Northern Railway. Abandoned in 1960.
		Chisholm, Virginia	15		1899-1902			Absorbed into Great Northern in 1902.
Tower Logging Co.	Tower Logging Railway Co.	Murray	22.5		1895-1905	2/R	2/G 140	Operated off Duluth & Iron Range
Trout Lake Lumber Co.	Trout Lake Lumber Co.	Lake Vermilion	2.5		1902-1906	1/R	10	Portage railroad. (**)
		Lake Vermilion	3		1915-1918			Portage railroad. (**)
Virginia & Rainy Lake Co. (*)	Virginia & Rainy Lake	Lake Junction	20	50	1902-1911	5/R	5/G 200	Railroad operated by Minnesota Land & Construction Co. Line west of Lake Junction abandoned in 1911. Off DV&RL.
		Cusson	140	1422	1911-1929	9/R	5/G 360	Logging lines operated by V&RL. Cusson off DRL&W (DW&P).
		Kinmount	7		1908-1910			Logging lines operated by V&RL, off DRL&W.
		Arbutus (DW&P)	10		1909-1915			Logging Lines operated by V&RL.
		Gooseberry	20		1909-1912	1/R	2/G	Logs delivered to Duluth & Northern Minnesota.
White Cedar Timber Co.	White Cedar Timber Co.	Big Falls	33		1923-1937	2/R	1/G-1	Also known as Twomey-Williams Co., off M&I.

Abbreviations:

BN – Burlington Northern
D&IR – Duluth & Iron Range
D&NE – Duluth & Northeastern
DM&N – Duluth, Missabe & Northern
DRL&W – Duluth, Rainy Lake & Winnipeg

DW&P – Duluth, Winnipeg & Pacific
GN – Great Northern
M&I – Minnesota & International
M&R – Merrill & Ring
NP – Northern Pacific
SOO – Minneapolis, St. Paul & Sault Ste. Marie

(*) See also Minnesota Land & Construction Co.
(**) Isolated railroad operation

D   Diesel Locomotive
G-1 Gasoline operated locomotive
G   Geared locomotive
R   Rod locomotive

183

LIMA SHAY GEARED LOCOMOTIVES
USED IN MINNESOTA

Construction Number	Date Built	Cylinder and Driver — Dimensions	Minnesota Lumber Operator	Remarks
164	1887	10x10 — 28	J. M. Paine & Co. "Lizzie"	Sold to Washington & British Columbia
173	1887	10x10 — 29	Duluth & Northeastern No. 13	From B. F. Hazelton, Pennsylvania
–	–	– –	Northern Mill Co. No. 1	3-foot gauge (old engine)
321	1890	10x12 — 29½	Northern Mill Co. No. 3	3-foot gauge, to National Iron Works
368	1891	8x12 — 26	C. N. Nelson Lbr. Co. No. 2	To Mesabe Southern, became D&NE No. 10
397	1892	10x10 — 28	Mitchell & McClure No. 3	
417	1892	10x10 — 28	Mitchell & McClure No. 4	To John Hein & Co., Wisconsin, to various operators in Arkansas
551	1898	12½x12 — 36	Virginia & Rainy Lake Co. No. 22	From F. A. Blackwell No. 4, to North Bend & Kettle Creek No. 4, to Lake Superior Piling No. 4, to Minnesota Lake & Construction No. 22, to Virginia & Rainy Lake No. 22
637	1901	11x12 — 32	Red River Lumber Co. No. 4	Former Nebagamon Lbr. Co. No. 4
–	–	– –	Tower Lumber Co. No. 1	
693	1901	10x12 — 29½	Tower Lumber Co. No. 2	Sold to Oregon Operator
769	1903	11x12 — 32	Minnesota Land & Construction No. 20	To Virginia & Rainy Lake No. 20
770	1903	12x12 — 32	Minnesota Land & Construction No. 21	To Virginia & Rainy Lake No. 21
1506	1905	12x15 — 36	Minnesota Land & Construction No. 23	To Virginia & Rainy Lake No. 23
1522	1905	8x8 — 26½	Consumers Ore Co. No. 1	To Houghton Lumber Co.
1523	1905	8x8 — 26½	Consumers Ore Co. No. 2	To Alabama lumber firm
1589	1905	10x12 — 29½	Consumers Ore Co. No. 3	
1592	1905	10x12 — 29½	Consumers Ore Co. No. 4	To Hanna Mining Co.
1703	1906	12x15 — 36	Minnesota Land & Construction No. 24	To Virginia & Rainy Lake No. 24, to Hudson Bay Mining & Smelting, Canada
1815	1907	8x10 — 26½	Nichols-Chisholm Lumber Co. No. 2	To Mississippi lumber firm
1819	1907	12x15 — 36	Corrigon McKinney Co. No. 11	To General Logging Co. No. 80
1858	1907	10x10 — 29½	Shenango Furnace Co. No. 1	To Wisconsin lumber firm
1859	1907	10x10 — 29½	Shenango Furnace Co. No. 2	To Great Fall Montana lumber firm
1861	1907	10x10 — 29½	Shenango Furnace Co. No. 4	To Shelvin Clarke Ltd.
1862	1907	10x10 — 29½	Shenango Furnace Co. No. 5	To Park Falls Lumber Co.
1863	1907	10x12 — 29½	Shenango Furnace Co. No. 6	To Alabama Power Co. No. 4
1908	1907	12x15 — 36	Alger-Smith Lumber Co. No. 101	To Duluth & Northern Minnesota No. 101, to Maryland firm
2006	1908	13½x15 — 36	Corrigan & McKinney Co. No. 12	To General Logging No. 82
2197	1909	13½x15 — 36	Corrigan & McKinney Co. No. 16	To General Logging No. 83
–	–	– –	Swallow & Hopkins No. 3 (1st)	Former Cranberry Lumber No. 3 (old engine)
2226	1909	11x12 — 32	Swallow & Hopkins No. 1	To Cleveland Cliffs Iron Co.
2227	1909	11x12 — 32	Swallow & Hopkins No. 2	To Cleveland Cliffs Iron Co.
2239	1909	11x12 — 32	Swallow & Hopkins No. 3 (2nd)	To Cleveland Cliffs Iron Co.
2240	1909	11x12 — 32	Swallow & Hopkins No. 4	To Cleveland Cliffs Iron Co.
2341	1910	10x12 — 29½	Pine Tree Mfg. Co. No. 20	To Crookston Lumber Co. To Louisiana
2376	1910	12x15 — 36	Pine Tree Mfg. Co. No. 2	To Potlatch Lumber Co. No. 105
2573	1912	10x12 — 29½	Crookston Lumber Co. No. 4	To Wilton & Northern No. 4, to British Columbia
2625	1912	10x12 — 29½	Crookston Lumber Co. No. 5	To Wilton & Northern No. 10, to Washington
2644	1913	10x12 — 29½	Crookston Lumber Co. No. 6	To Wilton & Northern No. 6, to Washington
2665	1913	10x10 — 29	Nichols-Chisholm Lumber Co. No. 4	To Crookston Lumber Co., to Connor Land & Lumber Co., to Laona & Northern
2717	1913	11x12 — 32	Duluth & North Eastern No. 18	
2733	1913	10x12 — 29½	Crookston Lumber Co. No. 4	To Washington state lumber firm
3259	1925	10x12 — 29½	Built for International Lumber Co.	Became Minnesota, Dakota & Western 2nd No. 1

BRAINERD & NORTHERN MINNESOTA RAILWAY

Number	Type	Builder and Construction Number		Date Built	Drivers	Dimensions – Cylinders –	Weight	Disposition and Remarks
1	2-6-0	Baldwin	12890	1892	50	15x24	70,660	Named *Josephine*. Became M&I No. 1 in 1901.
2	2-6-0	Baldwin	12957	1892	50	15x24	70,660	Named *James B. Ransom*. Became M&I No. 2 in 1901.
3	2-6-0	Baldwin	14338	1895	50	14½x24	72,000	Became M&I No. 3. Sold to A. Guthrie & Co. in 1906.
4	2-6-0	Baldwin	14339	1895	50	14½x24	72,000	Became M&I No. 4. Retired 1926.
5	2-6-0	Richmond	2722	1898	56	18x26	115,000	Original No. 23. Became M&I No. 5. Leased to MD&W 1917-1920. Retired in 1926.
6	2-6-0	Richmond	2723	1898	56	18x28½x26	115,000	Original No. 24. Became M&I No. 6. Retired 1926. Built with cross-compound cylinders.
7	2-6-0	Richmond	2829	1899	62	18x28½x26	115,000	Became M&I No. 7. Leased to Twomey-Williams in 1924. Built with cross-compound cylinders. Retired in 1929.
8	2-6-0	Richmond	2830	1899	62	18x28½x26	115,000	Became M&I No. 8. Retired in 1926. Built with cross-compound cylinders.
9	2-6-0	Richmond	3122	1900	57	18x28½x26	115,000	Became M&I No. 9. Sold to Twomey-Williams in 1926. Built with cross-compound cylinders.
10	2-6-0	Richmond	3123	1900	57	18x28½x26	115,000	Became M&I No. 10. Sold in 1926. Built with cross-compound cylinders.
23	2-6-0	Richmond	2722	1898	56	18x26	115,000	Renumbered B&NM No. 5.
24	2-6-0	Richmond	2723	1898	56	18x28½x26	115,000	Renumbered B&NM No. 6.

Abbreviations: B&NM – Brainerd & Northern Minnesota Railway
M&I – Minnesota & International Railway
MD&W – Minnesota, Dakota & Western Railway

Note: Brainerd & Northern Minnesota record for 1893 indicate ownership of three 22-ton Forney type locomotives of which there is no further reference. *Poor's Manual of Railroads* for 1895 states that the road owned ten locomotives, six of which cannot be accounted for in the above roster. These were presumed to have been secondhand motive power. It is possible that these locomotives may have been owned by parent Minnesota Logging Co. and used in their logging operation.

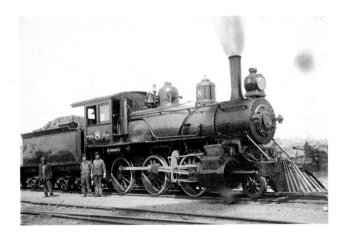

Minnesota & International cross-compound No. 8 was built by Richmond for the Brainerd & Northern Minnesota in 1899 as their No. 8. — WAYNE C. OLSEN COLLECTION (BELOW) No. 23 was also built by Richmond for the B&NM. She was renumbered to No. 5 in 1898, the same year she was built. — FRANK KING COLLECTION

NORTHERN MILL CO. - GULL LAKE & NORTHERN RAILWAY

Number	Type	Builder and Construction Number		Date Built	Dimensions Drivers —	Cylinders —	Weight	Disposition and Remarks
1	Shay	Lima	–	–				Early 3-foot gauge Shay.
2	2-6-0	Baldwin	–	–				3-foot gauge locomotive
3	Shay	Lima	321	1890	29½	10x12	93,000	2-truck Shay 3-foot gauge. Sold to National Iron.

Note: Northern Mill Company (Gull Lake & Northern Railway) is a predecessor of Brainerd & Northern Minnesota.

DULUTH & NORTHEASTERN RAILROAD

Number	Type	Builder and Construction Number		Date Built	Dimensions Drivers —	Cylinders —	Weight	Disposition and Remarks
(1st) 1	4-4-0	Rogers	2929	1882	63	17x24	89,000	Ex StP&D No. 17, exDL&C No. 17, became D&NE No. 4.
(2nd) 1	2-6-0	Cooke	41117	1906	54	19x24	133,680	
2	2-6-0	Porter	2599	1902	42	15x24	81,700	
(1st) 3	2-6-0	Porter	2591	1902	42	15x24	81,700	Became D&NE No. 19.
(2nd) 3	2-6-0	Cooke	41118	1906	54	19x24	133,680	
4	4-4-0	Rogers	2929	1882	63	17x24	89,000	1st D&NE No. 1, originally StP&D No. 17.
5	4-4-0	Brooks	1104	1886	59	17x24		Ex NP No. 1109 (StP&D No. 40). Received in 1906.
6	4-6-0							Ex MStP&A
7	4-6-0							Ex MStP&A
8	2-8-0							Ex MStP&A
9	2-6-0							
10	Shay	Lima	368	1891	26	8x12	39,000	Ex C. N. Nelson No. 2, ex Mesabe Southern No. 2.
11	4-4-0							Ex MStP&A
12	2-8-0	Baldwin	11214	1890	50	20x24	116,800	Ex CNE&W No. 28, CNE No. 28, ex MS No. 4. Scrapped in 1924. Boiler used at D&NE Cloquet roundhouse.
13	Shay	Lima	173	1887	29	10x10	70,000	From B. F. Hazelton.
14	2-8-0	Baldwin	40875	1913	51	20x24	144,500	Sold to Black Hills Central — South Dakota.
15								No data or information.
16	2-8-0	Baldwin	40874	1913	51	20x24	144,500	On display at Cloquet
17	2-6-0	Porter	1625	1895	42	14x24	70,000	Ex C. N. Nelson, ex MS No. 3.
18	Shay	Lima	2717	1913	32	11x12	120,000	
19	2-6-0	Porter	2591	1902	42	15x24	81,700	1st D&NE No. 3.
20	2-6-0	Baldwin	30260	1907	54	19x24	124,000	Ex Panama No. 330. Originally 5-foot gauge.
21	2-6-0	Baldwin	30217	1907	54	19x24	124,000	Ex Panama No. 325. Originally 5-foot gauge.
22	2-8-0	Pittsburgh	1525	1894	50	22x28	160,000	Ex DM&N No. 300.
23	2-8-0	Pittsburgh	1563	1895	50	22x28	160,000	Ex DM&N No. 301.
24	2-8-0	Baldwin	33897	1909	50	20x24	144,000	Ex V&RL No. 18.
25	2-8-0	Baldwin	33898	1909	50	20x24	144,000	Ex V&RL No. 19
26	0-6-0	Baldwin	26958	1905	51	21x26	160,000	Ex WM No. 1003, ex GC&E No. 103, to PRR No. 17 in 1945, to D&NE in 1952.
27	2-8-0	Pittsburgh	42286	1907	56	22x28	204,000	Ex DM&IR No. 348, on display at Barnum, Minnesota.
28	2-8-0	Pittsburgh	39587	1906	56	22x28	204,000	Ex DM&IR No. 332. On display at Lake Superior Transportation Museum, Duluth, Minnesota.
29	0-6-0	Lima	8381	1944	50	21x28	157,300	Ex U.S. War Dept. No. 4047, ex BT No. 123.
30	0-6-0	Alco	62894	1921	50	21x26	160,000	Original Winston-Dear No. 123, ex EM, ex LST&T No. 21.
31		EMD				600 hp.		Ex EJ&E, to D&NE in 1964.
32		EMD				600 hp.		Ex EJ&E, to D&NE in 1964.
33		EMD				600 hp.		Ex EJ&E, to D&NE in 1965.
34		EMD				1000 hp.		Ex EJ&E, to D&NE in 1965.
35		EMD		1968		1000 hp.		Acquired New.

Abbreviations:
BT — Bay Terminal of Toledo
CNE — Central New England
CNE&W — Central New England & Western
DL&C — Duluth Log & Contracting
DM&IR — Duluth, Missabe & Iron Range
DM&N — Duluth, Missabe & Northern

EJ&E — Elgin, Joliet & Eastern
EM — Evergreen Mining
GC&E — Greenbrier, Cheat & Elk
LST&T — Lake Superior Terminal & Transfer
MStP&A — Minneapolis, St. Paul & Ashland

MS — Mesabe Southern
NP — Northern Pacific
PRR — Preston Railroad
StP&D — St. Paul & Duluth
V&RL — Virginia & Rainy Lake
WM — Western Maryland

The Duluth & Northeastern's 2nd No. 1 was built by Cooke in 1906. The original No. 1 had been purchased secondhand and became No. 4. — FRANK KING COLLECTION

No. 6 was rented to the Hines Lumber Co. for use in western Douglas County, Wisconsin, when this photograph was taken, circa 1908. — HOWARD PEDDLE COLLECTION

No. 2 was built by Porter in 1902. The engine was near the end of her career when this photo was taken. — HAROLD VAN HORN

No. 7 was acquired from the Minneapolis, St. Paul & Ashland, a Weyerhaeuser logging railroad located in nearby northern Wisconsin. — FRANK KING COLLECTION

Mogul No. 3 was the second engine to carry this number. She poses here on a log train somewhere north of Duluth. — DARWIN JANKE COLLECTION

The Baldwin Locomotive Works built Consolidation type No. 14, along with sister No. 16, in 1913. These were the last steam locomotives built for the D&NE. — FRANK KING

No. 16 was built by Baldwin in 1913 for the D&NE. Note the three single-stage air pumps. The engine is now on display in Cloquet. — FRANK KING

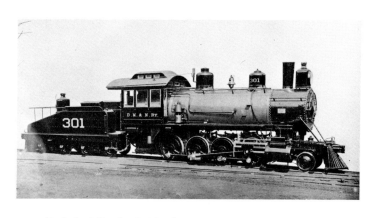

Duluth, Missabe & Northern No. 301 was identical to No. 300. She became Duluth & Northeastern No. 23. —FRANK KING COLLECTION

Locomotive No. 21 was built to 5-foot gauge for service in building the Panama Canal. She was in switching service when this photograph was taken. —HAROLD VAN HORN

The Baldwin Locomotive Works built D&NE No. 24 which originally was Virginia & Rainy Lake Co. No. 18 — HAROLD VAN HORN

D&NE No. 22 was built as Duluth, Missabe & Northern No. 300. Her long rear boiler overhang made her prone to derailments on the D&NE. — FRANK KING COLLECTION

Duluth & Northeastern No. 25 was formerly Virginia & Rainy Lake No. 19. She was built by Baldwin in 1909 for the V&RL. — FRANK KING

This husky Consolidation was the last steam locomotive operated by the D&NE. No. 28 was former Missabe Road No. 332 and is now on display at the Lake Superior Museum of Transportation at Duluth. — FRANK KING

No. 26 was received by the Duluth & Northeastern in 1952. She was built by the Baldwin Locomotive Works in 1905 as Western Maryland No. 1003. — FRANK KING

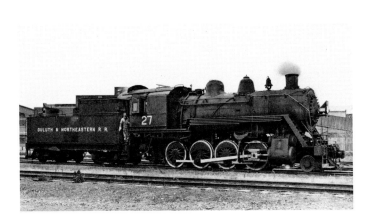

Lima built No. 29 in 1944 for the U.S. War Department. On the D&NE she was used for industrial switching at Cloquet. — FRANK KING

Duluth & Northeastern No. 27 was built for the Missabe Road in 1907 as their No. 348. She is now on display at Barnum, Minnesota. — FRANK KING

Lake Superior Terminal & Transfer No. 21 became D&NE No. 30. She was the last steam locomotive acquired by the D&NE. — FRANK KING

DULUTH & NORTHERN MINNESOTA RAILWAY

Number	Type	Builder and Construction Number		Date Built	Dimensions Drivers — Cylinders —		Weight	Disposition and Remarks
1	2-6-0	Baldwin	11092	1890	50	16x24		Built as Manestique No. 3 (Alger-Smith of Michigan). Became D&NM No. 1, to Helena Land & Lumber, Arkansas.
2	2-6-0	Baldwin	6649	1883	52	16x24	75,000	From D&IR No. 3 in 1899. On exhibit at Two Harbors.
(1st) 3	2-6-0	Baldwin				16x24		Ex Illinois Central, scrapped in 1909.
(2nd) 3	4-6-0	Baldwin	33338	1909	56	19x26		Sold to Escanaba & Lake Superior No. 15.
4	2-6-0	Baldwin	8441	1887	57	17x24	90,000	Ex AT&SF No. 0198, No. 356. Received in 1902.
5	2-6-0	Baldwin	8445	1887	48	18x24	90,000	Original Gulf, Colorado & Santa Fe Nos. 72, 355, 0197.
6	2-6-0	Baldwin			48	18x24	90,000	
7	2-6-0	Brooks	1938	1891	42½	14x22		Purchased from Mitchell & McClure No. 2 in 1902.
8	2-8-0	PRR	327	1876	50	20x24	92,720	Ex PRR No. 164, secured from Mitchell & McClure No. 5 in 1902. Sold to Hermansville & Western.
9	2-8-0	Baldwin	1783	1868	49	20x24	93,300	Ex Union Pacific No. 1250. Acquired 1904 from Hicks. First 2-8-0 on U.P.
10	4-6-0	Baldwin	29645	1906	56	19x26		Sold to John Kaiser Lbr, to Dells Pulp & Paper.
11	4-6-0	Baldwin	29721	1906	56	19x26		Sold to Escanaba & Lake Superior No. 16.
12	4-6-0	Baldwin	32166	1907	56	19x26		Sold to Houghton, Chassel & Southwestern, to Ontonagon Railroad.
13	2-8-2	Baldwin	39664	1913	51	20x28	180,100	Sold in 1919 to Lake Superior & Ishpeming No. 21, Renumbered No. 15.
14	2-8-2	Baldwin	39665	1913	51	20x28	180,100	Sold in 1919 to Lake Superior & Ishpeming No. 22, Renumbered No. 14. Sold to Inland Stone Div. of Inland Steel. Preserved at Lake Superior Transportation Museum.
101	Shay	Lima	1908	1907	36	12x15	130,000	To Kendall Lumber, sold 1929 to Stanley Coal Co. (Preston Railway)

Note: Locomotive No. 8 was built by the Pennsylvania Railroad at their Altoona Shops as a Class I (H1).

Duluth & Northern Minnesota No. 1 had seen previous service on the logging lines of Alger-Smith in Michigan. — WAYNE C. OLSEN COLLECTION (UPPER RIGHT) No. 2 photographed in front of the enginehouse at Knife River was built for the nearby Duluth & Iron Range as their No. 3 in 1883. — LAKE COUNTY HISTORICAL SOCIETY (RIGHT) D&IR's famed *Three Spot* as she appears today on exhibit at Two Harbors, Minnesota. The first engine on the road, she was used to handle work trains during the construction period. — BASGEN PHOTO

190

No. 6 on the ready track at Knife River roundhouse. The engine appears she is fresh out of the backshop. —DENNIS OJARD COLLECTION

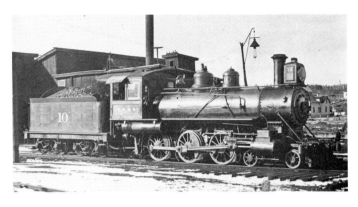

Locomotive No. 10 was one of four identical Ten Wheelers built by Baldwin for the D&NM. The engine reposes here in front of the enginehouse at Knife River. — FRANK KING COLLECTION

No. 9 was built by Baldwin in 1868 as Union Pacific No. 113 and later re-numbered No. 1250. She had the distinction of being the first 2-8-0 on the UP. — GERALD M. BEST COLLECTION

Mikado type No. 14 of the D&NM as she appeared on the ore-carrying Lake Superior & Ishpeming. The D&NM sold the engine to the LS&I in 1919. FRANK KING COLLECTION

The Lake Superior & Ishpeming purchased D&NM No. 13 in 1919 and numbered the engine No. 21. The LS&I later renumbered the engine to No. 15 as shown in this scene. — WAYNE C. OLSEN

DULUTH, MISSISSIPPI RIVER & NORTHERN RAILROAD

Number	Type	Builder and Construction Number		Date Built	Dimensions Drivers — Cylinders — Weight			Disposition and Remarks
1	2-6-0	Porter	1346	1892	40	12x18	51,000	Received from Wells-Stone Co.
2	2-6-0	Porter	1353	1892	48	14x24	64,000	Received from Wells-Stone Co.
3	2-6-0	Brooks	2205	1892	44	14x22	63,000	Sold to Swan River Logging in 1893. See Note 1.
4	2-6-0	Brooks	2273	1893	50	16x24	85,000	Sold to Swan River Logging in 1894. See Note 2.
5	2-6-0	Brooks	2274	1893	50	16x24	85,000	Sold to Swan River Logging in 1894.
6	2-6-0	Brooks	2430	1894	44	14x24	63,000	
7	2-6-0	Brooks	2535	1895	51	18x24	96,000	Sold to Swan River Logging.
8	2-6-0	Brooks	2967	1898	51	18x24	110,500	See Note 3.
9	4-6-0	Brooks	2968	1898	63	18x24	127,800	See Note 3.
10	2-8-0	Baldwin				20x24		Sold

Note 1 — Locomotive No. 3 was eventually sold to the Birmingham Rail & Locomotive Co. who rebuilt the engine. It was then sold to the Big Sandy Lumber Co. in 1919.

Note 2 — Locomotive No. 4 was also sold to the Birmingham Rail & Locomotive Co. After rebuilding it was sold to Hemphill Lumber Co. in 1920 as their No. 4.

Note 3 — Sold to A. Guthrie & Co. Locomotive No. 9 became St. Louis, Memphis & Southeastern No. 698. Later became Frisco No. 698 and then No. 2698.

DMR&N Mogul No. 3 was built by Brooks in 1892. Note the five-slotted drawbar pocket which was necessary to accommodate the varying coupler heights on logging cars used at the time. — ALCO HISTORIC PHOTOS

DMR&N No. 7 arrived in Minnesota from Brooks during 1895. She was later sold to the Swan River Logging Company sometime during the 1890's. —ALCO HISTORIC PHOTOS

Engine No. 4 was similar to No. 3 with the exception of larger cylinders and driving wheels. She was rebuilt by the Birmingham Rail & Locomotive Co. and sold to the Hemphill Lumber Co. of Kennett, Missouri, as their No. 4. — ALCO HISTORIC PHOTOS

Ten Wheeler No. 9 became St. Louis, Memphis & Southeastern No. 698, and later Frisco No. 698 and No. 2698. — FRANK KING COLLECTION

DULUTH, RAINY LAKE & WINNIPEG RAILWAY

Number	Type	Builder and Construction Number		Date Built	Drivers —	Dimensions Cylinders —	Weight	Disposition and Remarks
100	4-6-0	Rogers	41210	1906	62	19x26	143,000	Became DW&P No. 910, No. 1352, CN No. 1352, scrapped in 1929.
101	4-6-0	Rogers	41211	1906	62	19x26	143,000	Became DW&P No. 911, No. 1353, CN No. 1353.
200	2-8-0	Rhode Island	40678	1906	50	20x26	154,000	Became DW&P No. 921, No. 2005, CN No. 1800, scrapped in 1925.
201	2-8-0	Rhode Island	40679	1906	50	20x26	154,000	Became DW&P No. 922, No. 2006, CN No. 1801, scrapped in 1934.
202	2-8-0	Rhode Island	40680	1906	50	20x26	154,000	Became DW&P No. 923, No. 2007, CN No. 1802, scrapped in 1927.
900	2-6-0	Dickson	26261	1902	56	19x26	129,000	Ex DV&RL No. 10.
901	2-6-0	Dickson	26263	1902	56	19x26	129,000	Ex DV&RL No. 12.
902	2-6-0	Dickson	26264	1902	56	19x26	129,000	Ex DV&RL No. 13.
905	0-6-0	Schenectady	48354	1910	50	19x26	124,000	Became DW&P No. 336, CN No. 7066, scrapped in 1936.
924	2-8-0	Schenectady	48352	1910	50	20x26	156,000	Became DW&P No. 2008, CN No. 1803.
925	2-8-0	Schenectady	48353	1910	50	20x26	156,000	Became DW&P No. 2009, CN No. 1804.

Abbreviations: CN — Canadian National
DV&RL — Duluth, Virginia & Rainy Lake
DW&P — Duluth, Winnipeg & Pacific

No. 924 came to the DRL&W from Schenectady in 1910 and was kept busy during her early years hauling log trains into Virginia, Minnesota. She later became DW&P No. 2008 and later Canadian National No. 1803. — FRANK KING COLLECTION

Duluth, Rainy Lake & Winnipeg Consolidation type No. 202 was built by Rhode Island in 1906. She later went to the Duluth, Winnipeg & Pacific and eventually became Canadian National No. 1802. — ALCO HISTORIC PHOTOS

DULUTH, VIRGINIA & RAINY LAKE RAILWAY

Number	Type	Builder and Construction Number		Date Built	Drivers —	Dimensions Cylinders —	Weight	Disposition and Remarks
1	2-6-0	Porter	2536	1902	48	16x24	90,000	To Virginia & Rainy Lake No. 1.
2	2-6-0	Porter	2537	1902	48	16x24	90,000	To Virginia & Rainy Lake No. 2.
3	2-6-0	Porter	3545	1906	48	16x24	90,000	To Virginia & Rainy Lake No. 3.
10	2-6-0	Dickson	26261	1902	56	19x26	129,000	To DRL&W No. 900 in 1910, to CN No. 484.
11	2-6-0	Dickson	26262	1902	56	19x26	129,000	Sold to M&NW in 1906.
12	2-6-0	Dickson	26263	1902	56	19x26	129,000	To DRL&W No. 901 in 1910, to DW&P No. 128, to CN No. 485.
13	2-6-0	Dickson	26264	1902	56	19x26	129,000	To DRL&W No. 902 in 1910, to DW&P No. 129, to CN No. 486. See Note.
14	2-6-0	Dickson	26288	1903	56	19x26	129,000	Taken off the roster in 1906.
15	2-6-0	Dickson	26289	1903	56	19x26	129,000	Sold to Detroit, Toledo & Ironton No. 69.

Note: Locomotive No. 13 sold to C. H. Sharp Construction Co., later became Sharp & Fellows Construction Co. No. 7. Converted to a 2-6-2. Now on display at Travel Town, Griffith Park, Los Angeles.

Locomotives Nos. 10, 12 and 13 were transferred to the Duluth, Rainy Lake & Winnipeg.

Abbreviations: CN — Canadian National
DRL&W — Duluth, Rainy Lake & Winnipeg
DW&P — Duluth, Winnipeg & Pacific
M&NW — Minnesota & North Wisconsin

Sharp & Fellows Construction Co. No. 7, now on display at Traveltown in Los Angeles, was formerly Duluth, Virginia & Rainy Lake No. 13. Built as a Mogul, the 1902 Dickson-built engine was converted to a 2-6-2 by Sharp & Fellows. —GERALD M. BEST

GENERAL LOGGING COMPANY

Number	Type	Builder and Construction Number		Date Built	Drivers	— Cylinders —	Weight	Disposition and Remarks
22	4-6-0	Pittsburgh	1841	1898	56	19x26	123,000	Ex Duluth, Missabe & Northern No. 22.
24	4-6-0	Pittsburgh	1958	1899	56	19x26	123,000	Ex Duluth, Missabe & Northern No. 24.
29	4-6-0	Pittsburgh	2094	1900	56	19x26	123,000	Ex Duluth, Missabe & Northern No. 29.
33	4-6-0	Pittsburgh	2098	1900	56	19x26	123,000	Ex Duluth, Missabe & Northern No. 33.
80	Shay	Lima	1819	1907	36	12x15	160,000	3-Truck Shay, ex Corrigan-McKinney Co. No. 11.
81	Heisler	Heisler	1533	1926	38	17x15	160,000	Ex Pine Run Coal Co. No. 81, sold to BR&L, to Alabama Shipbuilding & Drydock in 1942.
82	Shay	Lima	2006	1908	36	13½x15	160,000	Ex Corrigan-McKinney Co. No. 12.
83	Shay	Lima	2197	1909	36	13½x15	160,000	Ex Corrigan-McKinney Co. No. 16.
90	2-8-2	Lima	5438	1917	51	22x28	250,000	Ex Cambria & Indiana No. 7.
91	2-8-2	Lima	5574	1917	51	22x28	250,000	Ex Cambria & Indiana No. 8.

Duluth, Missabe & Northern No. 24 was sold to the Northern Lumber Co. in 1923. She later became General Logging Co. No. 24. — HOWARD PEDDLE COLLECTION (UPPER RIGHT) General Logging Shay No. 80 awaiting the scrappers torch at Duluth during November 1936. — JOHN GRANFORS (RIGHT) Heisler No. 81 was built during 1926 for the Pine Run Coal Company. — FRANK KING COLLECTION

MESABE SOUTHERN RAILWAY

Number	Type	Builder and Construction Number		Date Built	Drivers	Dimensions — Cylinders —	Weight	Disposition and Remarks
1	4-4-0							Ex C. N. Nelson No. 1 — an old locomotive.
2	Shay	Lima	368	1891	26	8x12	39,000	Ex C. N. Nelson No. 2, to Duluth & Northeastern No. 10.
3	2-6-0	Porter	1625	1895	42	14x24	70,000	To Duluth & Northeastern No. 17.
4	2-8-0	Baldwin	11214	1890	50	20x24	116,800	Ex CNE&W No. 28, to Duluth & Northeastern No. 12.
5	2-6-0							No information.
6								No information.

Abbreviations: CNE&W — Central New England & Western

MINNEAPOLIS & RAINY RIVER RAILWAY

Number	Type	Builder and Construction Number		Date Built	Drivers	Dimensions — Cylinders —	Weight	Disposition and Remarks
1	2-6-0	Porter	1291	1891	42	14x20	64,000	Ex Itasca Railroad No. 1.
2	2-6-0	Porter	2952	1898	42	14x22	74,000	Ex Itasca Railroad No. 2. Sent to Joyce Operations in Louisiana.
3	4-4-0							Ex Itasca Railroad No. 3.
4	2-6-0						80,000	Ex Minneapolis & St. Louis.
5	4-4-0	Danforth		1869	62	16x24	60,500	Ex Milwaukee Road No. 140, No. 1206. Acquired in 1904. Note 1.
6	4-4-0						90,000	Ex Northern Pacific.
7	4-6-0	Dickson	37527	1905	56	18x24	122,000	
8	2-6-0	Cooke	40221	1906	54	19x24	124,000	See Note 2.
9	2-6-0	Cooke	40222	1906	54	19x24	124,000	See Note 2.
10	2-6-0	Cooke	40223	1906	54	19x24	124,000	See Note 2.
11	4-4-0							
12	4-4-0						75,000	

Note 1 — Named *L.P. Morten* of Milwaukee & St. Paul Railroad.

Note 2 — Built to specifications of locomotives used in construction of the Panama Canal.

Little Minneapolis & Rainy River Mogul No. 1 was retired when this photograph was taken. She was built by Porter in 1891 for the Itasca Railroad, a predecessor of the M&RR. — FRANK KING COLLECTION (UPPER RIGHT) Itasca Railroad No. 2 was built by Brooks in 1898. She became No. 2 on the Minneapolis & Rainy River in 1901. — FRANK KING COLLECTION (RIGHT) Locomotive No. 10 was on the scrap line at Duluth when this photograph was taken. This is the locomotive appearing on the title page color view. — HAROLD VAN HORN

MINNEAPOLIS, RED LAKE & MANITOBA RAILWAY

Number	Type	Builder and Construction Number		Date Built	Drivers	Dimensions – Cylinders –	Weight	Disposition and Remarks
1	0-4-4	Baldwin		1892	42	9x15x16		Ex Chicago South Side Elevated, ex Red Lake Trans No. 1.
2	2-6-0							Acquired from Hicks.
3	2-6-0	Porter						Ex Red Lake Transportation No. 3.
4	4-6-0	Baldwin	37568	1912	56	17x24		Purchased new. Scrapped at Duluth in 1939.
5	4-6-0	Baldwin	39396	1913	56	16x24		Ex Bloomsburg & Sullivan No. 8, acquired from Southern Iron & Equipment in 1929 as their No. 2264.

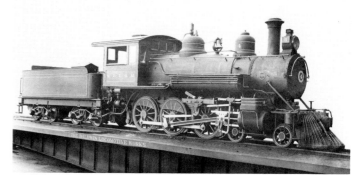

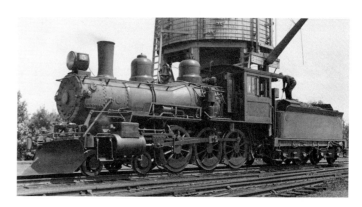

Minneapolis, Red Lake & Manitoba No. 3 at Redby. At the time of this photograph the engine's diamond stack had been replaced by a Gooch style smokestack. — FRANK KING COLLECTION (UPPER RIGHT) Ten Wheeler No. 4, with a capped stack, arrived from the Baldwin Locomotive Works in 1912. — BROADBELT COLLECTION (RIGHT) Snowplow equipped No. 5 was acquired by the MRL&M in 1929. She was built by Baldwin for the Bloomsburg & Sullivan of New Jersey as No. 8 in 1913. — HAROLD VAN HORN COLLECTION

MINNESOTA & NORTH WISCONSIN RAILROAD

Number	Type	Builder and Construction Number		Date Built	Drivers	Dimensions – Cylinders –	Weight	Disposition and Remarks
1	Heisler	Heisler	1060	1902			74,000	2-truck Heisler purchased new. Sold to Kentwood & Eastern (Brooks-Scanlon Lumber Co.)
9	2-6-0				48	17x22		Built as tank engine — equipped with a tender. Likely former Delaware Lackawanna & Western.
11	2-6-0	Dickson	26262	1902	56	19x26	129,000	Ex Duluth, Virginia & Rainy Lake. No. 11
12	4-4-0	Baldwin	2514	1871				Ex West Wisconsin No. 12, ex Chicago, St. Paul, Minneapolis & Omaha No. 12. To Scanlon-Gipson in 1898.
105	4-4-0	Baldwin	6176	1882	63	17x24		Ex Great Northern No. 105, St. Paul, Minneapolis & Manitoba No. 105.
291	2-6-0	Dickson	354	1882	57	18x24	97,572	Ex Delaware, Lackawanna & Western No. 291, No. 30. Acquired from Hicks in 1902.
296	2-6-0	Cooke	1386	1882	57	18x24	97,572	Ex Delaware, Lackawanna & Western No. 43, No. 305, No. 296. Acquired in 1903.
1208	4-4-0	Taunton	430	1869	62	13x22	60,500	Ex Mineral Point *Platteville*, ex Chicago, Milwaukee & St. Paul No. 430 No. 1208. Acquired in 1901.
—	0-4-0							No information.

MINNESOTA, DAKOTA & WESTERN RAILWAY

Number	Type	Builder and Construction Number		Date Built	Drivers	Dimensions — Cylinders —	Weight	Disposition and Remarks
(1st) 1	2-6-0							No information.
(2nd) 1	Shay	Lima	3259	1925	29½	10x12	93,200	Ex International Lumber
(1st) 2	2-6-0	Alco						No information.
(2nd) 2	Heisler	Heisler	1549	1927	33	14x22	110,000	Ex International Lumber No. 2, to Lehigh Coal & Navigation in 1935.
3	2-8-0							No information.
4								No information.
5	0-6-0	Baldwin	39392	1913	50	19x24	112,600	
6	4-6-0	Baldwin	33034	1908	57	19x26		Ex Keweenaw Central No. 20.
7	0-6-0	Baldwin	10452	1889	49	19x24		Used in International Bridge & Terminal Co. service. Ex Joliet & Blue Island No. 23.
8	0-6-0	Pittsburgh	2122	1900	50	19x26	120,450	Ex Duluth, Missabe & Northern No. 56. Acquired in 1920.
9	0-6-0	Pittsburgh	2123	1900	50	19x26	120,450	Ex Duluth, Missabe & Northern No. 57. Acquired in 1920.
10	0-8-0	Baldwin	59892	1927	51	21x28		Used in International Bridge & Terminal Co. service. Sold to Algers, Winslow & Western No. 10.
101	2-8-0	Baldwin	39393	1913	56	20x26	147,800	
102								No information.
103	2-8-0	Baldwin	44500	1916	56	20x26	151,000	

Note: Minnesota, Dakota & Western Railway locomotives were also operated over the rail lines of parent company the International Lumber Company.

International Lumber Co. Shay No. 1 was built in 1925. She saw service on the Red Lake spurs and on International's big operation out of International Falls. — MINNESOTA HISTORICAL SOCIETY

Ten Wheeler No. 20 of the copper carrying railroad Keweenaw Central was later to become Minnesota, Dakota & Western No. 6. — BROADBELT COLLECTION

Lehigh Navigation Coal Company's Heisler No. 120 was built for the International Lumber Company in 1927 as their 2nd No. 2. — BENJAMIN F. G. KLINE, JR. COLLECTION.

MD&W 0-6-0 switcher No. 8 simmers in the summer sun at International Falls in 1947. This engine and sister No. 9 were built by Pittsburgh in 1900 for the Missabe Road. — FRANK KING

Eight-coupled switcher No. 10 was the newest steam locomotive on the MD&W, arriving from Baldwin in 1927. She spent most her years in International's bridge service. — BROADBELT COLLECTION

Consolidation No. 103, along with sister No. 101, handled most of the main line work over International Lumber Co. lines and the Minnesota, Dakota & Western. — BROADBELT COLLECTION

MITCHELL & McCLURE LOGGING RAILROAD

Number	Type	Builder and Construction Number		Date Built	Dimensions Drivers — Cylinders —		Weight	Disposition and Remarks
1	2-6-0			1891				No information.
2	2-6-0	Brooks	1938	1891	42½	14x22		Sold to Duluth & Northern Minnesota in 1902 as No. 7.
3	Shay	Lima	397	1891	28	10x10		
4	Shay	Lima	417	1892	28	10x10		Sold to John Hein & Co., to Little Rock Lumber & Manufacturing, to Bemberg & Son Iron Works, to Helena, Parkin & Northern RR.
5	2-8-0	PRR	327	1876	50	20x24	92,720	Built by Altoona Shops as No. 164, sold to D&NM in 1902 as No. 8, to Hermansville & Western RR.

VIRGINIA & RAINY LAKE COMPANY

Number	Type	Builder and Construction Number		Date Built	Dimensions Drivers — Cylinders —		Weight	Disposition and Remarks
1	2-6-0	Porter	2536	1902		16x24	90,000	Original Duluth, Virginia & Rainy Lake No. 1.
2	2-6-0	Porter	2537	1902		16x24	90,000	Original Duluth, Virginia & Rainy Lake No. 2.
3	2-6-0	Porter	3545	1906		16x24	90,000	Original Duluth, Virginia & Rainy Lake No. 3.
9	2-6-0				36			Small engine called *Goose*. Reputed to have been narrow-gauge from Hines operation at Cusson, Wisc.
14	2-8-0	Baldwin	39670	1913	50	20x24	144,000	Became Lake Superior Lumber.
15	2-8-0	Baldwin			50	20x24	91,640	Ex PRR, acquired from Washburn & Northwestern No. 22 of Edward Hines Lumber Co.
16	2-8-0	Baldwin			50	20x24	91,640	Ex PRR, acquired from Washburn & Northwestern No. 20 of Edward Hines Lumber Co.
17	2-8-0	Baldwin	33896	1909	50	20x24	144,000	Used at Virginia Mill.
18	2-8-0	Baldwin	33897	1909	50	20x24	144,000	Became Duluth & Northeastern No. 24.
19	2-8-0	Baldwin	33898	1909	50	20x24	144,000	Became Duluth & Northeastern No. 25. See Note.
20	Shay	Lima	769	1903	32	11x12	120,000	Ex Minnesota Land & Construction Co. No. 20.
21	Shay	Lima	770	1903	32	12x12		Ex Minnesota Land & Construction Co. No. 21. See Note.
22	Shay	Lima	551	1898	36	12½x12		Ex T. A. Blackwell No. 4, Lake Superior Piling No. 4. See Note
23	Shay	Lima	1506	1906	36	12x15		Ex Minnesota Land & Construction Co. No. 23.
24	Shay	Lima	1703	1906	36	12x15	160,000	Ex Minnesota Land & Construction Co. No. 24, to Hudson Bay Mining & Smelting (Canada).

Note: These locomotives also used by Virginia & Rainy Lake at their Split Rock operation off the Duluth & Northern Minnesota.

Porter-built Virginia & Rainy Lake Mogul No. 3 at Virginia. Note the stack is covered as the locomotive is up for sale. She was acquired from the Duluth, Virginia & Rainy Lake. — FRANK KING COLLECTION

Consolidations Nos. 18 and 19 saw additional years of service on the Duluth & Northeastern becoming their Nos. 24 and 25. The two 72-ton engines were built by Baldwin in 1909 for the Virginia & Rainy Lake. — FRANK KING COLLECTION

Veteran engine No. 15 came to the VR&L from the Washburn & Northwestern a Hines logging railroad in northern Wisconsin. The engine ended her long career with the closing of the mill in 1929 and she was scrapped in Duluth. — FRANK KING COLLECTION

Shay No. 22 was the nomad of the V&RL fleet. She was built in 1898 for T. A. Blackwell No. 4, then North Bend & Kettle Creek No. 4, Lake Superior Piling No. 4, Minnesota Land & Construction No. 22 and finally V&RL No. 22. — FRANK KING COLLECTION

Consolidation No. 16, along with sister engine No. 15, was built for the Pennsylvania Railroad during the 1880's. She also worked on the Hines operation in Wisconsin before coming to the V&RL. — FRANK KING COLLECTION

Three-truck Shay No. 23 was built by Lima in 1906 for the Minnesota Land & Construction Co. This husky hill climber weighing 70 tons became Virginia & Rainy Lake No. 23. — FRANK KING COLLECTION

The Baldwin Locomotive Works built No. 16 for the V&RL in 1909 for main line log service. Later, she was assigned to work as the mill switcher at Virginia. — BROADBELT COLLECTION

BIBLIOGRAPHY

Books

Adams, Kramer. *Logging Railroads of the West.* Seattle: Superior Publishing Co., 1961.

Bryant, Ralph Clement. *Logging.* New York: John Wiley & Sons, Inc., 1914.

Carter, James L. *Voyageurs Harbor.* Grand Rapids: Pilot Press, 1967.

Casler, Walter and Taber, Thomas T, III. *Climax: An Unusual Locomotive.* Morristown: Railroadians of America, 1960.

Hidley, Ralph W., Hill, Frank E., and Nevins, Allan. *Timber and Men: The Weyerhaeuser Story.* New York: The Macmillan Co., 1963.

Hoar, Walter G. *History is Our Heritage.* Shell Lake: White Birch Printing Co., 1968

Holbrook, Stewart H. *Holy Old Mackinaw.* New York: The Macmillan Co., 1942.

Horn, Stanley F. *This Fascinating Lumber Business.* New York: Bobbs-Merrill Co., 1943.

Johnston, Hank. *They Felled the Redwoods.* Los Angeles: Trans Anglo Books, 1960.

King, Frank A. *The Missabe Road.* San Marino: Golden West Books, 1972.

Koch, Michael. *The Shay Locomotive: Titan of the Timber.* Denver: World Press, 1971.

Krenz, Duane. "The Virginia & Rainy Lake Co.," Unpublished Manuscript, 1968.

Labbe, John T. and Goe, Vernon. *Railroads in the Woods.* Berkeley: Howell-North Books, 1961.

Martin, Albro. *James J. Hill and the Opening of the Northwest.* New York: Oxford University Press, 1976.

Nute, Grace Lee. *Rainy River Country.* St. Paul: Minnesota Historical Society, 1960.

Ochler, C. M. *Time in the Timber.* St. Paul: Minnesota Historical Society, 1948.

Poor's Manual of Railroads. New York: H. V. and H. W. Poor Publishing Co., 1886-1920.

Pyle, Joseph G. *The Life of James J. Hill.* New York: Doubleday, Doran & Co., 1915.

Rector, William Gerard. *Log Transportation in the Lake States Lumber Industry 1840-1918.* Glendale: The Arthur H. Clark Co., 1953.

Ryan, J. C. *Early Loggers in Minnesota* (Volume I). Duluth: Minnesota Timber Producers Assn., 1973.

Ryan, J. C. *Early Loggers in Minnesota* (Volume II). Duluth: Minnesota Timber Producers Assn., 1976.

Van Brunt, Walter. *Duluth and St. Louis County* (Volumes 1-3). Chicago: American Historical Society, 1921.

Vandersluis, Charles. *Mainly Logging.* Minneota: Minneota Clinic, 1974.

Woodbridge, Dwight E. *History of Duluth and St. Louis County* (Volumes 1-2). Chicago: C. F. Cooper & Co., 1910.

Newspapers

Chippewa Herald, Chippewa Falls, Wisconsin, 1883.

Dispatch, Brainerd, Minnesota, December 19, 1890.

News Tribune, Duluth, Minnesota, 1886-1930

Trade Periodicals

American Lumberman

Mississippi Valley Lumberman

General Periodical Articles

Hagg, Harold P. "Logging Line: A History of the Minneapolis, Red Lake and Manitoba." *Minnesota History,* Winter 1972.

King, Frank A. "Logging Railroads in Northern Minnesota." Bulletin No. 93, Railway & Locomotive Historical Society, October 1955.

Records and Reports

Annual Reports of the Cloquet Lumber Co., 1899-1903.

Annual Report of the International Lumber Co., 1930.

Annual Reports of the Northern Lumber Co., 1899-1903

Annual Report of the Split Rock Lumber Co., 1906.

Duluth, Winnipeg & Pacific Railway records pertaining to dealings with the Virginia & Rainy Lake Co.

Minnesota Railroad and Warehouse Commission files and annual reports.

"Scenes in the Virgin Forest: Logging Camps and Manufacturing Plant of the Virginia & Rainy Lake Co." Virginia & Rainy Lake Co., 1924.

Virginia & Rainy Lake Co. articles of incorporation.

INDEX

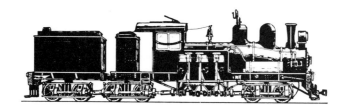